Educating Young Children With and Without Exceptionalities

A volume in
Contemporary Perspectives in Special Education
Anthony F. Rotatori and Festus E. Obiakor, *Series Editors*

CONTEMPORARY PERSPECTIVES IN SPECIAL EDUCATION

Anthony F. Rotatori and Festus E. Obiakor, *Series Editors*

Leadership Matters in the Education of Students with Special Needs in the 21st Century (2017)

> edited by Festus E. Obiakor, Tachelle Banks, Anthony F. Rotatori, and Cheryl Utley

Critical Issues in Preparing Effective Early Childhood Special Education Teachers for the 21st Century Classroom: Interdisciplinary Perspectives (2016)

> edited by Festus E. Obiakor, Alicja Rieger, and Anthony F. Rotatori

Multicultural Education for Learners with Special Needs in the Twenty-First Century (2014)

> edited by Festus E. Obiakor and Anthony F. Rotatori

Autism Spectrum Disorders Inclusive Community for the 21st Century (2012)

> edited by Julie Deisinger, Sandra Burkhardt, Timothy J. Wahlberg, Anthony F. Rotatori, and Festus E. Obiakor

Educating Young Children With and Without Exceptionalities

New Perspectives

edited by

Festus E. Obiakor
Sunny Educational Consulting

Tachelle Banks
Cleveland State University

Jessica Graves
College of Coastal Georgia

Anthony F. Rotatori
St. Xavier University

INFORMATION AGE PUBLISHING, INC.
Charlotte, NC • www.infoagepub.com

Library of Congress Cataloging-in-Publication Data

A CIP record for this book is available from the Library of Congress
http://www.loc.gov

ISBN: 978-1-64113-593-1 (Paperback)
       978-1-64113-594-8 (Hardcover)
       978-1-64113-595-5 (ebook)

LIST OF CONTRIBUTORS

Bob Algozzine, PhD
Distinguished Professor Emeritus
University of North Carolina, Charlotte
Charlotte, North Carolina

Eugene Asola, PhD
Associate Professor, Physical Education
Valdosta State University
Valdosta, Georgia

Jeffrey P. Bakken, PhD
Associate Provost of Academic Affairs
and Dean of Graduate School
Bradley University
Peoria, Illinois

Tachelle Banks, PhD
Chairperson and Professor
Department of Teacher Education
Associate Vice President of Institutional
  Diversity
Cleveland State University
Cleveland, Ohio

Floyd Beachum, PhD
Bennett Professor of Education
Program Coordinator of Educational
  Leadership
Lehigh University
Bethlehem, Pennsylvania

Emily C. Bouck, PhD
Professor, Special Education
Michigan State University
East Lansing, Michigan

Sarah Byrnes
Graduate Doctoral Student
Michigan State University
East Lansing, Michigan

Bridgie Alexis Ford, PhD
Professor, Special Education
University of Akron
Akron, Ohio

Lenwood Gibson, PhD
Associate Professor of Special
  Education
Queens College, City University
  of New York
New York City, New York

Jessica B. Graves, PhD
Chair and Associate Professor
College of Coastal Georgia
Brunswick, Georgia

Mateba K. Harris, PhD
Assistant Principal
Thurgood Marshall High School
Fort Bend Independent School District
Missouri City, Texas

Cindy Nelson Head, PhD
Assistant Professor, Special Education
University of West Georgia
Carrollton, Georgia

Ying Hui-Michael, PhD
Chair and Professor of Special
  Education
Rhone Island College
Providence, Rhode Island

Edgar X. Jordan, PhD
Adjunct Professor, School Psychology
Springfield College (Milwaukee
  Campus)
Milwaukee, Wisconsin

Kalli Kemp, PhD
Assistant Professor, Special Education
Rhode Island College
Providence, Rhode Island

Lynn Kline, PhD
Associate Professor, Early Childhood
  Education
University of Akron
Akron, Ohio

Alan Livingston, EdS
Milwaukee Public Schools, School
  Psychologist
Milwaukee, Wisconsin

Stephanie T. Marshall, PhD
Adjunct Instructor, Special Education
Grand Canyon University
Phoenix, Arizona

Carlos McCray, PhD
Associate Professor, Educational
  Leadership
University of Louisville
Louisville, Kentucky

Sunday O. Obi, EdD
Professor of Education
Kentucky State University
Frankfort, Kentucky

Festus E. Obiakor, PhD
Chief Executive Manager
Sunny Educational Consulting
Shorewood, Wisconsin

Beth Pinheiro, PhD
Assistant Professor, Special Education
Rhode Island College
Providence, Rhode Island

Anthony F. Rotatori, PhD
Emeritus Full Professor, Psychology
St. Xavier University
Chicago, Illinois

Sonya Sanderson, DA
Associate Professor, Physical Education
Valdosta State University
Valdosta, Georgia

Emma Sipila
Graduate Doctoral Student
Michigan State University
East Lansing, Michigan

Ramel L. Smith, PhD
D&S Healing Center
Milwaukee, Wisconsin

Reverend Maurice Stinnett, EdD
Vice President of Diversity, Inclusion,
  and Culture
Brooklyn Sports Entertainment Global
Brooklyn, New York

Shaunita D. Strozier, PhD
Associate Professor, Special Education
Valdosta State University
Valdosta, Georgia

Alana Telesford
Graduate Student, School Psychology
College of Education
Lehigh University
Bethlehem, Pennsylvania

Shernavaz Vakil, EdD
Professor, Special Education
University of Akron
Akron, Ohio

Sean Warner, PhD
Professor, College of Education
Clark Atlanta University
Atlanta, Georgia

CONTENTS

FOREWORD

In the last decade, we have seen a proliferation of Hollywood blockbuster superhero action movies. Of course, the superhero genre has always been a part of our cinematic fabric. In fact, it goes as far back as 1941; and since that time, we have seen multiple versions of movies about Superman, Batman, Spiderman, and The Hulk. Last year, Wonder Woman opened to global acclaim earning close to $500 million; and now with great anticipation, we have Black Panther gracing the big screen in a few days (not to mention the Black Lightning and Luke Cage projects on Netflix). We have finally arrived at a place where the diversity of our society is being represented in our superheroes and it's truly a wonderful thing. Yet, we are still behind when one considers the reverberating political noise of hegemony, misogyny, and xenophobia in the United States of America and the world over.

What I have always enjoyed about the superhero storylines is the notion of a common person possessing extraordinary powers and gifts. Most of the stories depict an ordinary person living an ordinary life who, from childhood, was perpetually castigated, misunderstood, disparaged, or disenfranchised in some way. Often, they were afraid to display their talents showing their true selves for fear of further ridicule and derision. Years later as an adult or young adult, they realize that their powers and abilities make them special human beings; beings that actually have the power to help human society to be better than what it is or espouses to be.

My favorite was the X-Men, mainly because they were a diverse collective of individuals who although different all had parallel experiences of being ostracized and demeaned at a young age. Essentially, their story is that their

Educating Young Children With and Without Exceptionalities, pages ix–xii
Copyright © 2019 by Information Age Publishing
ix

tremendous abilities were defined as abnormalities of the human biology—a mutation. I identified strongly with this narrative because my experiences as a young child coming to this country in 1974 country were full of moments of insecurity and embarrassment because of the myriad ways I was treated differently. I too felt very much like a mutant, which is the actual language used to characterize the X-Men in the story. And like the mutants, I felt like my talents and/or abilities actually served as barriers to belonging and acceptance. Moreover, these gifts were overlooked and not viewed as strengths that teachers could use to improve my learning, their practice, or the learning of others.

It might be the reason why young children identify so viscerally with superheroes, especially the ones that actually look like them. The fact is young children do not frame their realities as disadvantaged or disabled regardless of their physical, social, or emotional challenges. They see themselves as beings with powers and talents. What is even more heartening is that young children generally embody a limitless capacity to learn and love. I know I did, despite the disrespect and incivility I faced as a little brown second-grader with a funny accent and funny clothes.

The challenge for school personnel then and now remains centered around ensuring the creation of classroom and school conditions that embrace the allowance of young children to be their full selves in ways that promote harmony and excellence. In the X-Men story the mutant children actually had their own school—a space where they could be accepted and celebrated for who they were and wanted to become. As the narrative illustrates, the founder, Charles Xavier who also had special telepathic powers made it his mission to seek out these children and founded Xavier's School for Gifted Youngsters. It was a place where young children learned to read and write while learning how to control their powers and foster friendly human-mutant relationships.

Forty-three years later, in spite of the overwhelming body of knowledge associated with holistically educating young children with and without exceptionalities, our educational system and preparation programs continue to harbor elements of misidentification, misdiagnosis, miscategorization, misplacement, and miseducation. My own misdiagnosis and miscategorization, started from second through sixth grade and laid the groundwork for my own internalized oppression. Each day after being introduced to my second grade teacher, Mrs. V, I was subjected to a form of kryptonite that was especially made for me—one that caused me to question my own abilities and self-worth. Slowly a new reality was being constructed, one that changed me from a boy with boundless possibilities and dreams to one with aspirations of just getting by. My special powers and gifts were eroding away. And, at such a young age, I was not outfitted with the proper faculties to articulate what was happening. I did not know how to advocate for myself while enduring the constant bombardment of skewed daily messaging that was sapping my talents, and transforming me from superhero to mutant and finally to something else; something I did not recognize, understand or like.

What was missing then and still missing now, for young children like me, was an acknowledgment of the significance and importance of the powerbrokers in this narrative; and the power that they have to intervene to potentially change the storyline. By powerbroker, I mean teachers, curriculum specialists/coaches, guidance counselors, principals, assistant principals, and superintendents. Many know they have the power to change the outcomes of young children from all walks of life but need the appropriate support, time, resources, and freedom to innovate in the spaces they control. And, those who are not as informed, the ones I encountered in P.S. 34 in Queens, need to move beyond their own cultural blindness to recognize the complexity and diversity of abilities their students possess. That is why this new book, *Educating Young Children With and Without Exceptionalities: New Perspectives* by Obiakor, Banks, Graves, and Rotatori is so critical. This text offers those in and preparing to enter the teaching profession clear and cogent instruction and guidance to leverage the talents young children (and their families) bring to the classroom. Furthermore, it challenges us to stretch beyond what we know and how we utilize what know in educating young children with and without exceptionalities. It asks us to embrace the discomfort associated with applying pedagogical innovations, collaborating with families, and transforming educator preparation programs. Most importantly, it provides a blueprint for school leaders passionate about creating learning environments that support authentic teacher and counselor voice as well as families and community stakeholders.

In his recent CNN interview with Van Jones, the rap artist turned businessman Jay Z, who is now worth 810 million dollars, intimated that people need to be treated like human beings. He asserted that paying someone well and denigrating them does not equate with happiness. Thus, Obiakor, Banks, Graves, and Rotatori and the contributors in this text seek to transform conventional thinking and behaviors associated with educating young children with and without exceptionalities such that all are seen, instructed, supported, guided, and heard in ways that affirm their humanity. In that same interview, Jay Z in his allegorical representation of the "superbug" asserts that we have tacitly normalized the structural oppression of certain people by "spraying perfume over the garbage in the trash can" rather than dealing with the garbage, therefore, allowing the garbage and the bugs (the tools of oppression and dehumanization) to produce a superbug, an entity that has been fortified and validated over time and now must be dealt with. And that is what *Educating Young Children With and Without Exceptionalities* attempts to do—call us to action to deal with the superbug. Put another way, the book urges us to critically excavate our own professional conditioning relative to the language and tools we use when educating young children with and without exceptionalities.

A cursory etymological examination surrounding the word *exceptionality* suggests that its origins are grounded in terms that speak to the possession of superior and extraordinary skills, gifts, and/or strengths. Yet, that is not what is often conjured up in the minds of many when talking about the education of young children, particularly those who have been historically disenfranchised. Obiakor, Banks, Graves, and Rotatori's book sets a course for us in that regard; awakening a new spirit of optimism in educating young children with talents and abilities.

Finally, this text requires, *the willing*, to renew their commitment to the acknowledgment and study of the gifts young children bring to the classroom. Additionally, the book challenges us to fervently examine the degree to which the sociocultural assets young children have can guide policy and practice in schools, educator preparation, and regulatory agendas. Essentially, Obiakor, Banks, Graves, and Rotatori have given us a comprehensive guide towards engendering and sustaining school climates that enable young children with and without exceptionalities to feel and behave like superheroes, every day.

—**Sean S. Warner, EdD**
Professor and Former Dean
School of Education
Clark Atlanta University
Atlanta, GA

PREFACE

Early childhood education (ECE) has always been intertwined with the use of developmentally appropriate practice (DAP). To support excellence in ECE, it is critical to the knowledge about individual children and child development principles combined with knowledge of effective early learning practices. Effective early childhood education involves an interdisciplinary collaborative process that is influenced by many factors. We present these aforementioned realities in *Educating Young Children With and Without Exceptionalities: New Perspectives*. In addition, we argue that general and special educators need to focus on applying new knowledge to better address critical issues that advance the field of educator preparation and improve educational outcomes for young children.

Early childhood research confirms the need for intensive intervention and remedial education—We need to avoid approaches that are "too little" or "too late." Also proven to yield positive results for children are practices familiar to early childhood educators. These practices include relationship-based teaching and learning; partnering with families; adapting teaching for children from different backgrounds and for individual children; active, meaningful, and connected learning; and smaller class sizes. Evidence of the benefits of these practices suggests that they should be extended more widely into the elementary grades.

Public policy and education reform influence issues and trends in how educators provide services to young children. Federal and state lawmakers realize that reaching children early is vital to closing achievement and opportunity gaps. The media spotlight shines on the establishment of public

Educating Young Children With and Without Exceptionalities, pages xiii–xv
Copyright © 2019 by Information Age Publishing
xiii

early learning initiatives highlighting better teacher training, assessment, and accountability standards. As a result, the new PreK–3 workforces must be well educated to be standards based on the latest research and sensitivity to cultural diversity. It is important to realize that fundamental to early childhood discipline is the utilization of developmentally appropriate, evidenced-based practices designed to meet the individual educational and socio-emotional needs of children and youth. To be effective, teachers must get to know each child well. The importance of teachers to high-quality early education, indeed to all of education, cannot be overemphasized. In the end, *Educating Young Children With and Without Exceptionalities* focuses on ensuring the creation of classroom and school conditions that embrace the allowance of young children to be their full selves in ways that promote harmony and excellence.

In this text, we invited dedicated scholars and educators who understand the plight of young children and youth who will later become our adults. This book is comprehensive in nature and provides researchers and practitioners with cutting-edge strategies. Chapter 1 discusses special education labels and the stigma associated with being defined by the label and subsequent performance deficits. This chapter responds to the ethical question of how we go beyond labels and deficits to provide appropriate education in the least restrictive environments for young children with and without exceptionalities. Chapter 2 establishes assessment as the engine behind special education placement and provision of instruction. The authors examine special education identification and placement processes and their impacts on standardized assessment and instruction. The chapter offers several suggestions to better identify and assess our young children. Chapter 3 provides an overview of the placement process of young students. The chapter focuses on how the potential of young children with exceptionalities can be maximized in all settings. Chapter 4 provides insight into how teachers at the elementary level can develop innovative teaching methods to teach diverse student populations—both students with and without disabilities. Chapter 5 focuses on effective ways in which school leaders can provide quality education to students with autism spectrum disorder or other children with disabilities. Chapter 6 highlights the reciprocal relationship between schools and families. The authors contend that there is a shared responsibility of ensuring that students obtain information and develop lifelong skills to live successfully in society. This chapter focuses on the importance of setting up interventions and resources for families beginning with early childhood programs that benefit all community members and stakeholders. The fundamental concepts addressed in Chapter 7 are community organizations, and school-community partnerships. The authors propose the *Comprehensive School–Community Partnership: Culturally Responsive* model to build networks and optimize the use of *significant multicultural community resources* (SMCR) that are traditionally marginalized as valuable resources. Chapter 8 identifies health and wellness, as critical aspects in the teaching and learning processes of young children. The authors respond to the ethical question of what can be done to foster the physical and mental health of young children. Chapter 9 discusses the use of technology to educate children with and without disabilities. Chapter 10 outlines the demand for highly effective educators of young children. The authors discuss current practices, challenges, and prospects in early childhood educator preparation programs. Chapter 11 examines historical trends, and current issues in the education of young children. In addition, it considers future directions for maximizing the potential of young learners with and without exceptionalities.

Finally, we thank our family members for their supports in this time-consuming venture. We also thank the professionals at Information Age Publishing for believing in us and our ideas. No doubt, a textbook of this nature cannot be successfully done without the collaboration, consultation, and cooperation of dedicated professionals who believe in change. We especially thank our contributors for sharing their perspectives and visions about educating young learners and preparing them for adulthood and life. We also thank Dr. Sean Warner of Clark Atlanta University for writing the Foreword.

—**Festus E. Obiakor**
Tachelle Banks
Jessica Graves
Anthony Rotatori

CHAPTER 1

EDUCATING YOUNG CHILDREN WITH AND WITHOUT EXCEPTIONALITIES

The Rationale

**Tachelle Banks, Festus E. Obiakor,
Anthony F. Rotatori, and Maurice Stinnett**

The history of educating students with exceptionalities in the United States parallels that of other groups in our society that have been excluded from services, and present future directions in education for students with and without exceptionalities. Programs for these students in the United States were made mandatory in 1975 when the U.S. Congress passed the Education for All Handicapped Children Act (EHA) in response to discriminatory treatment by public educational agencies against students with exceptionalities. The EHA was later modified to strengthen protections to people with exceptionalities and renamed the Individuals With Disabilities Education Act (IDEA, 2004). This federal law requires states to provide special education consistent with federal standards as a condition for receiving federal funds. IDEA entitles every student to a free and appropriate public

Educating Young Children With and Without Exceptionalities, pages 1–14
Copyright © 2019 by Information Age Publishing
1

education (FAPE) in the least restrictive environment (LRE). To ensure a FAPE, a team of professionals from the local educational agency usually meet with the student's parents to identify the student's unique educational needs, to develop annual goals for the student, and to determine the placement, program modification, testing accommodations, counseling, and other special services that the student needs. Parents become part of the multidisciplinary team, along with the local educational agency professionals, and collaborate with team members to make decisions on educational placement. These choices are recorded in a written Individualized Education Program (IEP). The school is required to develop and implement an IEP that meets the standards of federal and state educational agencies. Parents have the option of refusing special education services for their child.

Under IDEA, students with exceptionalities are entitled to receive special services through their local school district from Age 3 to Age 18 or 21. To receive special education services, a student must demonstrate a disability in one of 13 specific categories, including autism, developmental disability, specific learning disability, intellectual impairment, emotional and/or behavioral disability, intellectual disability, speech and language disability, deaf-blind, visual impairment, hearing impairment, orthopedic or physical impairment, other health impaired (including attention deficit disorder), and multiple exceptionalities and traumatic brain injury. Depending on the students' individual needs, they may be included, mainstreamed, or placed in a special school, and/or may receive many specialized services in resource rooms or self-contained classrooms. In addition to academic goals, the goals documented in the IEP may address self-care, social skills, physical therapy, speech therapy, and vocational training. Program placement is an integral part of the process, and typically takes place during the IEP meeting. To receive special education services disability definitions and labels are based on gaps and weaknesses in academic and social emotional performance as compared to students without exceptionalities. Disability labels can be stigmatizing as they follow students throughout their educational career. The stigma is associated with being defined by the label and subsequent performance deficits. How do we go beyond labels and deficits to provide appropriate education in the LREs for young children with and without exceptionalities? This chapter responds to this ethical question.

DEFICIT VERSUS DIVERGENCE: CONFLICTING CONSTRUCTS

The word "deficit" highlights inadequacy or insufficiency in student performance. It is defined as a deficiency or impairment in mental or physical functioning or an unfavorable condition or position; a disadvantage. The *deficit model* focuses on the student as the major problem, neither looking within the environment nor the instructional practices in the classroom. According to this model, the typical procedure is to test the student by determining eligibility for special education and then removing the student from the environment(s) where the problem existed. After more than two decades of federal legislation and implementation of the deficit model, there are now mounting concerns about the outcomes of students who have been served in this manner. Despite years of mandated services, many students with mild to moderate disabilities continue to be inadequately served, particularly African American children and youth who are disproportionally identified as having emotional behavior disorders or mild intellectual disabilities (Dunn, 1968; Harry & Klinger, 2007). For example, Harry and Klinger (2007) reviewed the recent history of special education and concluded that the focus on disability has become intertwined with the historical devaluing of CLD people in the United States and clearly, the deficit model influences the placement process of special education, resulting in a disproportionate placement of some CLD groups in special education.

On the other hand, "divergence" better qualifies students that receive special education services. The definition of divergence is a difference between two or more things. Divergence is also defined as a deviation from something such as a typical pattern or the process of separating or moving apart to follow different paths or different courses. Students who require special education display variation from typical developmental, learning, or behavioral patterns, resulting in the development of IEP that are designed to meet diverse learning needs. There is direct alignment between the definition of the divergence and the stated purpose of the IEP. To a large measure, divergence is different from deficit stance. Ironically, deficit highlights inadequacies that do not meet conventional educational expectations. The deficit model currently serves as the conceptual framework for placement in special education. Divergence highlights deviation from typical patterns without associated stigma for nonconformity. Schools should focus on differences rather than on deficits and should be concerned with finding instructional programs that work for challenging and at-risk children and youth. In the same vein, their teachers should monitor his or her own prejudices and carefully consider individual student variation as well as challenges before referring any student, particularly a CLD child, for special education.

Historically, the deficit model is based on the normative development of students whose homes and communities have prepared them for schooling long before they entered school. Children and youth from different social and cultural backgrounds begin the schooling process at a disadvantage because they deviate from majority social cultural norms and values. They begin school with different preparation and variation in home support of family members who establish and reinforce the goals of schooling. As a result, children and youth from different social and cultural backgrounds are expected to meet expectations that are qualitatively different from their developmental, social, and cultural structures (Obiakor, 2018). Consequently, under the auspices of the deficit model, students from different backgrounds quickly become candidates for suspected "disability." Considering the deficit model in concert with cultural variables strengthens the contention that students' lack of educational success is rooted in their cultures and communities. As previously discussed, the deficit model frames the problem as one of students and families. Instruction informed by deficit perspectives often fail to address problems within schools that depress the performance of certain groups of students. It is of no surprise that CLD children and youth continue to be overrepresented in special education, and limits access to the general education curriculum.

ACCESS TO THE GENERAL EDUCATION CURRICULUM

Access to the general education curriculum is an important issue for all students with exceptionalities, especially for CLD students (Skiba, Michael, Nardo, & Peterson, in press; Skiba, Peterson, & Williams, 1997). For example, the over-representation of African-American and Hispanic students in special education placements typically occurs in the categories of disability that are most subjective to identify, that is categories of mild cognitive disabilities, learning disabilities, and emotionally disordered (Donovan & Cross, 2002). Current findings suggest that the relationships among race, socioeconomic status (SES), and special education placement are highly complex, vary considerably by disability category, and are sometimes in a direction opposite to that expected. For the high-incidence disability categories, (e.g., cognitive disability), poverty appears to make a significant positive contribution to the disproportionate placement of students in special education programs (Oswald, Coutinho, Best, & Nguyen, 2001). For *serious emotional disturbance* (SED) however, African Americans are found to be overrepresented in low poverty districts (Oswald, Coutinho, Best, & Singh, 1999; Zhang & Katsiyannis, 2002).

To understand the significance of the issue of overrepresentation, it is critical to understand and address the broader context of American society and American education. Extensive research has been conducted to examine the (a) devastating effects of biological, social, and environmental factors (e.g., low birth weight, nutrition and development, fetal exposure to alcohol, tobacco or drugs, and exposure to lead) on the cognitive and behavioral functioning of CLD children (Donovan & Cross, 2002; Perner, 1991); (b) transactional nature of genetic and environmental influences on development (Donovan & Cross, 2002; Perner, 1991); (c) social and environmental factors related to low SES and the particular stressors associated with poverty (e.g., quality of parenting interaction, family interactions, language development, maternal depression, child care quality, and other risk factors; Donovan & Cross, 2002; Perner, 1991); and (d) the relationship between socio-demographic risk factors and academic deficits at school readiness. Clearly, school-related factors include: (a) recruitment and hiring of teachers with less experience and expertise in schools; (b) schools that are poorly funded, limited resources, and larger student-teacher ratios; (c) lowered teacher expectations by race or a cultural mismatch between expectations concerning CLD students' abilities; (d) denial of the existence of racial disparities in schools; and (e) structural disadvantages of schools (e.g., older, inadequate buildings, and out-of-date and insufficient supplies, curriculum, and equipment).

Some scholars attribute the overrepresentation of African-American and Hispanic students in special education to the use of identification tools such as intelligence tests, which are seen as culturally and linguistically biased (Losen & Orfield, 2002). For example, when Congress reauthorized IDEA in 1997, it added a provision requiring school districts to monitor the racial and ethnic breakdown of students receiving special education services. In the 2004 reauthorization, another provision was added to take the monitoring process further. Districts with an overrepresentation of CLD group members in special education must set aside 15% of their federal aid for students, particularly those in Grades K–3, who need "additional academic and behavioral support to succeed in a general education environment," according to the law. This reauthorization also required states to allow districts to use Response to Intervention (RTI), and "positive behavior support" (PBS) for determining if a child has a specific learning disability or behavioral disability. Response to Intervention involves early identification of students' learning problems and the use of increasingly intensive lessons, or interventions, to address those problems before they become entrenched (Samuels, 2011). The RTI three-tiered conceptual model is designed to shift the focus of educators on finding disability or within-child deficits to focusing on providing the best instruction for all children in the general education classroom. The RTI model emphasizes early intervention, with a focus on making sure children receive appropriate instruction at the "first tier" or classroom level, and the push to match instruction to a child's needs based on ongoing classroom assessment (Vaughn & Fuchs, 2003; Vaughn, Linan-Thompson, & Hickman, 2003; Vaughn, Mathes, Linan-Thompson, & Frances, 2005; Vellutino, Scanlon, Small, & Fanuele, 2003).

To a large measure, PBS includes (a) the development of positive behavioral expectations, (b) specific methods to teach these expectations to staff and students, (c) proactive supervision or monitoring of behaviors, (d) contingency management systems to reinforce and correct behavior, and (e) methods to measure outcomes and to evaluate progress across three tiers with specific core elements and these elements are (a) primary prevention/school-wide level, including universal school-wide management strategies to reduce disruptive behavior and teach prosocial skills to all students; (b) secondary prevention level, including targeted or group-based intervention strategies for students at risk of developing more serious antisocial behaviors (about 5% to 10%); and (3) tertiary prevention, including functionally derived treatment strategies for the small number of students (about 1%–3%) who engage in more chronic patterns of antisocial behavior (Horner, Crone, & Stiller, 2001; Horner, Sugai, & Lewis, 2005).

UNLOCKING EDUCATIONAL
DOORS: TOWARDS INCLUSIVE PRACTICES

The 1990s set the stage for a shift in special education. No longer were students with special needs separated from mainstream students (Praisner, 2003); instead, efforts were made to be inclusive in the education of general education classrooms. The literature has focused on the preparedness of educators and administrators to develop and utilize inclusion within their general education classrooms (Obiakor, Harris, Mutua, Rotatori, & Algozzine, 2012). In order for inclusion to be effective, there must be collaboration between special and general education teachers. However, these two teacher groups are not always effective in teaming together. Research has shown that teacher expectations influence student behavior, self-esteem, and achievement; therefore, if a teacher has a negative attitude toward students with exceptionalities, then they most likely will not be successful in his/her classroom (see Obiakor et al., 2012). Research has also shown that administrators' attitudes toward these students are important for successful inclusion, since they are able to develop and operate educational programs in their schools (Obiakor, Banks, Rotatori, & Utley, 2017). It has become clear that many school districts implement inclusion without adequate intervention or in-service training beforehand (see Obiakor et al., 2012; Obiakor, 2018).

Successful models of inclusion need to be analyzed and described. Researchers of peer-reviewed literature often write of the constructive impacts of inclusive education, focusing on the positive social skills learned by students, the sharpening of pedagogical skills, and the role of inclusive education in the promotion of civil rights (Broderick, Mehta-Parekh, & Reid, 2005; Polat, 2010; Soodak, 2003). Most importantly, research has shown how inclusive education also has an academic advantage for mainstream students. Soodak (2003) reviewed specific scenarios, whereas

Broderick et al. (2005) illustrated a broad picture of inclusive education. The literature focused on the necessity of teachers to receive training in inclusive education as part of their studies in becoming teachers (Florian & Linklater, 2010; Jordan, Schwartz, & McGhie-Richmond, 2009). Earlier, Daane, Beirne-Smith, and Latham (2000) examined administrators' and teachers' perceptions of the collaborative efforts of inclusion in the elementary grades. The study included 324 elementary general education teachers, 42 special education teachers, and 15 building administrators who were given surveys designed to address the Regular Education Initiative. The results showed that teachers and administrators both agreed that special and general education teachers worked together in planning IEPs. While collaboration is essential, the results revealed that collaboration was not a comfortable experience due to (a) conflict of personalities, (b) lack of planning time, and (c) limited time in the classroom by the special education teacher. Both general and special education teachers believed the inclusive classroom was not the most effective environment for students with exceptionalities, while administrators believed it was. For the teacher preparedness category, all interviewed individuals agreed that general education teachers were not prepared to teach students with exceptionalities. Although general education teachers seemed to be making good progress, they still lacked the confidence and support needed in dealing with these students. Both teachers and administrators believed students experienced social growth through the inclusion of students with exceptionalities in the classroom (Obiakor et al., 2017).

Idol (2006) described how special education services were provided in four elementary schools and four secondary schools within her program evaluation. In addition, she determined how often inclusion really occurred within the eight schools. The results indicated an inverse association between advances in inclusion and number of students identified as requiring special education services in the elementary schools. Therefore, the more advances the school made with inclusion, the fewer students identified as needing special education. However, the students could still be classified as at risk due to low test scores and low-income families. Only one elementary school included students with exceptionalities within the general education classroom 100% of the time. Some students at the other three elementary schools spent some time in the general education classroom; however, many spent less than 25% of their time or no time at all with their general education peers. Administrators were in favor of inclusion only if an instructional assistant or a special educator was present. All four elementary schools stated that they were applying the skills necessary for effective inclusion, which included (a) adaptation of instruction, (b) modification of curriculum, and (c) classroom management and student discipline. Elementary teachers recommended that professional programs be offered to teachers of students with exceptionalities and that mainstreaming be used over inclusion for students with more serious emotional problems.

For the secondary schools, it was shown that the number of students with exceptionalities varied more in the middle schools than in the high schools (Idol, 2006). However, there were more students with emotional disturbances at high schools than middle schools. In middle schools, most students with exceptionalities spent 100% of their time in the general education classroom. Not all high schools implemented inclusion. The high schools were more likely to implement alternatives to inclusion such as resource rooms or pull-out programs. In fact, in high schools, some students who had been referred for special education actually did not qualify for special education programs. All of the secondary school administrators were in favor of inclusion and had positive attitudes toward students with exceptionalities. However, they believed extra support should be available in the inclusive classroom for the teacher. Idol (2006) concluded that while the teachers believed they had the skills necessary for effective inclusion of students with exceptionalities (i.e., adaptation of instruction, modification of curriculum, classroom management, and student discipline), these skills were not consistently applied.

Earlier, Praisner (2003) examined attitudes of elementary school principals toward the inclusion of students with exceptionalities. This study was aimed at determining (a) the attitudes of elementary principals toward inclusion of students with exceptionalities, (b) how principals' personal and school characteristics as well as attitudes were related toward inclusion, and (c) how principals' perceptions of appropriate placements for students with different exceptionalities were related to their attitudes and experiences. Praisner (2003) found that a majority of principals did not have either a strongly positive or negative view toward inclusion; however, this majority generally skewed toward a positive attitude. A very small percentage had a clearly negative view toward inclusion. Principals favored inclusion when it was viewed as voluntary and generic and disfavored it when it was viewed as mandatory and specific. It was shown that principals chose full-time regular education with outside support for special education services.

FUTURE PERSPECTIVES

The challenges for school leaders seeking to successfully manage change are in creating conditions where what is known about "evidence-based practices" can be put to work to benefit children and youth. General education and special education teachers have continued to note concerns regarding the practical implementation of inclusion. Specifically, general education teachers doubt and resent the possibility of having children with special needs in their classrooms. The prospect of implementing the inclusive education model generates fear and resistance, mainly from teachers who are fearful of the training and support they will need to practice inclusion. Special educators are also fearful of inclusion. They are concerned that managers and administrators may see inclusion as a means to eliminate their jobs and save money. Others wonder if they have the knowledge and skills needed to assist general education teachers with inclusion.

The implementation of inclusive education needs to be a reflection of the successful relationship between collaborating teachers. The general education teacher needs to understand each special education student's IEP and prepare and execute lessons accordingly. Additionally, the collaborative teacher must be knowledgeable in the content area and in special education to ensure that every lesson's objectives are met. For example, teachers need to discuss IEPs and collectively develop strategies to properly implement differentiated education (Janney & Snell, 2006). Additionally, fieldwork and early exposure to inclusive education is beneficial in learning how and when to apply instructional modifications (Florian & Linklater, 2010). Most importantly, teachers must maintain a consistent and open relationship with parents. Keeping parents up to date with their children's progress is essential for a number of reasons; and the most important reason is to facilitate communication between the teacher and his/ her students effectively and maintain a positive relationship. An open rapport is important between parents and teachers so that the teachers are made aware if there is a problem outside of school. There are a number of methods a teacher can employ to effectively communicate with parents. Apart from traditional methods, such as email and phone conversations, weekly "newsletters" are sometimes used, and discussing group work and highlighting personal achievement frequently work. Other teachers send home handwritten notes to add a personal effect. A more regimented way is to have parents sign graded schoolwork and exams. Teachers need to decide what method works best for their learning environment. In addition to teacher responsibilities, administrators play a vital role in the successful implementation of inclusion (Obiakor et al., 2012; Obiakor et al., 2017).

Villa and Thousand's (2003) reiterated that administrators must take action to publicly articulate the new vision of inclusion, build consensus for the vision, and lead all stakeholders to active involvement. Principals must advance the integration, success, and acceptance of students with exceptionalities in order for inclusion to be successful. The attitudes of the principal can either increase or decrease inclusion opportunities for these students. In a study of 32 inclusive school sites, Villa and Thousand (2003) found that the degree of administrative support and vision was the most powerful predictor of general educators' attitudes toward inclusion. They concluded that administrators can provide four types of support for general and special educators, namely;

1. personal and emotional (being willing to listen to concerns),
2. informational (providing training and technical assistance),
3. instrumental (creating time for teachers to meet), and
4. appraisal (giving constructive feedback related to implementation of new practices).

Clearly, the implementation of inclusion may require a great deal of extra work for teachers and administrators. If inclusion is to be successful, leadership teams need to be established to assure that there are varied and systematic supports available for all teachers. In addition, it is important that school principals or directors become involved in the collaborative process of planning and review (Obiakor et al., 2017; Perner, 1991). In an inclusive environment, teachers' abilities should grow continually. Special education training helps teachers to teach to all levels, not just to those students with special needs. By logical extension, all future educators should build their pedagogical repertoire by making sure that inclusive practices be upheld (Obiakor et al., 2012).

Finally, teaching is a profession of ever-changing demands, and the need to develop and use new skills and approaches with students is considered essential. Teachers trained in isolation fail to produce significant transformations in the school culture (Blanco, 1999). Considerable evidence has indicated that both general and special educators feel inadequately prepared to serve students with exceptionalities in general education classrooms. Many general education teachers and leaders are not trained to provide diversified instructional methods (Obiakor et al., 2012; Roberts & Mather, 1995). To facilitate confidence and competence in the future, "teachers need systematic and intensive training that includes research-based best practices in inclusive schools" (Burstein, Sears, Wilcoxen, Cabello, & Spagna, 2004, p. 106). Teachers and educational leaders must engage in professional education as an ongoing part of their professional role (Fisher, Frey, & Thousand, 2003). Many areas of professional development are important, but research done by Fisher et al. (2003) stated that five high priority focus areas have futuristically emerged. These areas are: (a) collaborative teaming and teaching, (b) curricular and instructional modifications, (c) accommodations and personal supports, (d) assistive technology, and (e) positive behavioral supports.

If implemented properly, inclusive education services can: (a) be less expensive to implement and operate than special education services, (b) have a broader reach than traditional special education in terms of positive educational and social impacts on children, (c) contribute significantly to the ongoing professional development and job satisfaction of educators, and (d) produce better morale and team effort in the school environment. Legislative and policy provisions are important for the development of inclusive schools and supportive communities. The general principles must be backed up by operational strategies that get key officials and leaders to fully commit to implementing inclusion (Obiakor et al., 2012). If any area demands accountability, it is the education system that shapes our future as it shapes our children and youth. Clearly, quality indicators that inform what appropriate and effective inclusion in the future must include (a) leadership; (b) schools climate; (c) curriculum, instruction, and assessment; (d) program planning; (e) individual student support; (f) family–school partnerships; (g) collaborative planning; (h) professional development; and (i) planning for continued best practice improvement.

CONCLUSION

Segregated education has entrenched a way of thinking that tends to perpetuate the segregation of people with exceptionalities throughout their lives. Arguably, the systematic separation of certain people from the mainstream of society rips at the social fabric and dilutes the diversity of civil society as a whole. This has affected the education of young children with and without exceptionalities. We must be inclusive in our pedagogical practices. Inclusive education advances the cause of social justice and equity and supports the notion that all children should be provided a FAPE and educated in the LRE whether or not they have exceptionalities. The LRE mandate (IDEA, 2004) states that only students with extremely severe exceptionalities should be taught in separate special education classrooms; otherwise, students with exceptionalities should be taught and included in the general education classroom. This mandate is widely supported by parents, school professionals, researchers, and advocates of students with exceptionalities. Effective inclusive education requires sustained contact between the pedagogical specialist (special education teachers) and content specialists (general education teachers). All the success of an inclusive program cannot be entirely placed on the school system itself. Some pressure must also be placed on the individual teacher to do his/her part in making inclusion successful. Both general and special educators must be prepared to deal with students with exceptionalities. In addition, they must plan and implement the curriculum and, together, they must provide support to students with and without exceptionalities who need assistance (Roberts & Mather, 1995).

REFERENCES

Blanco, R. (1999). Towards schools for all with the involvement of all. In UNESCO's, *The major project of education* (pp. 80–84). Paris, France: UNESCO.

Broderick, A., Mehta-Parekh, H., & Reid, D. K. (2005). Differentiating instruction for disabled students in inclusive classrooms. *Theory Into Practice, 44*(3), 194–202.

Burstein, N., Sears, S., Wilcoxen, A., Cabello, B., & Spagna, M. (2004). Moving toward inclusive practices. *Remedial and Special Education, 25*(2), 104–116.

Daane, C. J., Beirne-Smith, M., & Latham, D. (2000). Administrators' and teachers' perceptions of the collaborative efforts of inclusion in the elementary grades. *Education, 121*(2), 331–338.

Donovan, M., & Cross, C. (2002). *Minority students in special and gifted education.* Committee on Minority Representation in Special Education. Washington DC: National Academy Press.

Dunn, L. (1968). Special education for the mildly retarded-is much of it justifiable? *Exceptional Children, 23,* 5–21.

Education for All Handicapped Children Act of 1975, 20 U.S.C. § 1400 et seq. (1975).

Fisher, D., Frey, N., & Thousand, J. (2003). What do special educators need to know and be prepared to do for inclusive schooling to work? *Teacher Education and Special Education, 26*(1), 42–50.

Florian, L., & Linklater, H. (2010). Preparing teachers for inclusive education: Using inclusive pedagogy to enhance teaching and learning for all. *Cambridge Journal of Education, 40*(4), 369–386.

Harry, B., & Klingner, J. K. (2007). Discarding the deficit model. *Educational Leadership, 64*(5), 16–21.

Horner, R. H., Crone, D. A., & Stiller, B. (2001). The role of school psychologists in establishing positive behavior support: Collaborating in systems change at the school-wide level. *NASP Communique, 29*(6). Retrieved from http://www.nasponline.org/publications/periodicals/spr/volume-29/volume-29-issue-3

Horner, R. H., Sugai, G., & Lewis, P. T. (2005). *School-wide PBS evaluation template.* Eugene, OR: University of Oregon.

Idol, L. (2006). Toward inclusion of special education students in general education. *Remedial & Special Education, 27*(2), 77–94.

Individuals With Disabilities Education Act of 1990, 1991, 1997, 1999, 20 USC §1400 et. seq. (statute); 34 CFR 300 (regulations), Regulations Implementing IDEA (1997) (*Federal Register,* 1999, March 12, 1999, vol. 64, no. 48).

Individuals With Disabilities Education Improvement Act of 2004, 20 USC § 1400 et seq.

Janney, R. E., & Snell, M. E. (2006). Modifying schoolwork in inclusive classrooms. *Theory Into Practice, 45*(3), 215–223.

Jordan, A., Schwartz, E., & McGhie-Richmond, D. (2009). Preparing teachers for inclusive classrooms. *Teaching and Teacher Education: An International Journal of Research and Studies, 25*(4), 535–542.

Losen, D., & Orfield, G. (2002). *Racial inequality in special education.* Cambridge, MA: The Civil Rights Project, Harvard Education.

Obiakor, F. E. (2018). *Powerful multicultural essays for innovative educators and leaders: Optimizing "hearty" conversation.* Charlotte, NC: Information Age.

Obiakor, F. E., Banks, T. I., Rotatori, A. F., & Utley, C. (2017). *Leadership matters in the education of students with special needs in the 21st century.* Charlotte, NC: Information Age.

Obiakor, F. E., Harris, M., Mutua, K., Rotatori, A., & Algozzine, B. (2012). Making inclusion work in general education classrooms. *Education and Treatment of Children, 35*(3), 477–490.

Oswald, D. P., Coutinho, M. J., Best. A. M., & Nguyen, N. (2001). Impact of sociodemographic characteristics on the identification rates of minority students as having mental retardation. *Mental Retardation, 39,* 351–367.

Oswald, D. P., Coutinho, M. J., Best, A. M., & Singh, N. N. (1999). Ethnic representation in special education. *Journal of Special Education, 32,* 194–206.

Perner, J. (1991). *Understanding the representational mind.* Cambridge, MA: MIT Press.

Polat, F. (2010). Inclusion in education: A step towards social justice. *International Journal of Educational Development, 31*(1), 50–58.

Praisner, C. L. (2003). Attitudes of elementary school principals toward the inclusion of students with disabilities. *Exceptional Children, 69*(2), 135–145.

Roberts, R., & Mather, N. (1995). The return of students with learning disabilities to regular classrooms: A sellout? *Learning Disabilities Research and Practice: A Publication of the Division for Learning Disabilities, Council for Exceptional Children, 10*(1), 46–58.

Samuels, C. A. (March, 2011). RTI: An instructional approach expands its reach. *Education Week, 30*(22), 2–5.

Skiba, R. J., Michael, R. S., Nardo, A.C., & Peterson, R. (2002). The color of discipline: Sources of racial and gender disproportionality in school punishment. *The Urban Review, 34,* 317–342. Retrieved from http://www.indiana.edu/~equity/docs/ColorofDiscipline2002.pdf

Skiba, R. J., Peterson, R. L., & Williams, T. (1997). Office referrals and suspension: Disciplinary intervention in middle schools. *Education and Treatment of Children, 20*(3), 295–315.

Soodak, L. C. (2003). Classroom management in inclusive settings. *Theory Into Practice, 42*(4), 327–333.

Vaughn, S., & Fuchs, L. S. (2003). Redefining learning disabilities as inadequate response to instruction: The promise and potential problems. *Learning Disabilities Research & Practice, 18,* 137–146.

Vaughn, S., Linan-Thompson, S., & Hickman, P. (2003). Response to instruction as a means of identifying students with reading/ learning disabilities. *Exceptional Children, 69,* 391–409.

Vaughn, S., Mathes, P., Linan-Thompson, S., & Frances, D. J. (2005). Teaching English language learners at risk for reading disabilities to read: Putting research into practice. *Learning Disabilities: Research & Practice, 20,* 58–67.

Vellutino, F. R., Scanlon, D. M., Small, S., & Fanuele, D. (2003, December). *Response to intervention as a vehicle for distinguishing between reading disabled and non-reading disabled children: Evidence for the role of kindergarten and first grade intervention.* Paper presented at the National Research Center on Learning Disabilities Responsiveness-to-Intervention Symposium, Kansas City, MO.

Villa, R. A., & Thousand, J. S. (2003). Making inclusive education work. *Educational Leadership, 61*(2), 19–23.

Zhang, D., & Katsiyannis, A. (2002). Minority representation in special education: A persistent challenge. *Remedial and Special Education, 23,* 180–187.

CHAPTER 2

IDENTIFICATION AND ASSESSMENT TOOLS FOR YOUNG CHILDREN

Ramel L. Smith, Edgar X. Jordan, and Alan Livingston

Derrick Bell (1992), the father of critical race theory, explored the intersection of race, law, power, ill-effects on disenfranchised, marginalized, and oppressed people in the society (Abdul-Jabbar, 2016; Coates, 2015; Hatcher, 2016; Kozol, 1991; Obiakor, Harris-Obiakor, & Smith, 2002). Sadly, young children are one of the most vulnerable groups, coupled with the inability to *solely* advocate for themselves. As a result, though many laws are proposed, created and enacted, we have yet to see sustained success on a mass level for all school-age children.

In the Office of Special Education and Rehabilitative Services report in 2010, the U.S. Department of Education proudly asserts that there has been progress in how schools viewed, educated, and treated students with recognized disabilities since 1975 with the Education for All Handicapped Children Act (EHA); Public Law 94-142. This law helped to end certain forms of discrimination as this law allowed all children, specifically those with

Educating Young Children With and Without Exceptionalities, pages 15–29
Copyright © 2019 by Information Age Publishing
All rights of reproduction in any form reserved.

15

disabilities, to receive a free and appropriate education (FAPE). This was monumental in the educational world, as it provided financial aid, proper educational assistance and protection for children and parents. In 1990, Individuals With Disabilities Education Act (IDEA) was revised to make this law more robust: (a) Birth–2 for families and 3–21 component for school aged ready children; (b) in conjunction with the FAPE, it was documented that this should be performed in the least restrictive environment (LRE); (c) creation of individualized education plans (IEP) were formed to create a measure to record concrete goals and measure the effectiveness of interventions designed to help the child increase academic and behavior skills; and (d) ensure financial viability with federal assistance to help sustain current programs and search out innovative techniques to continually employ the best options to maintain success for all children. Seven years later, the Individuals With Disabilities Education Improvement Act (IDEIA, 2004) was passed and beefed up to provide special education to children with disabilities.

While the laws have made a significant difference in the lives of millions of families over the past 40 years, Sailor and many other scholars believe the intent of EHA and subsequent amendments were followed to the letter of the law, but not the spirit of the law, as it created an entire different system (Rose & Meyer, 2006; Sailor, 2017; Smith & Sapp, 2005; Utley & Obiakor, 2001). As it appears, special education has been used as an educational weapon of mass destruction for populations that are: (a) Black and Brown, (b) from urban and rural areas, and (c) low socioeconomic status groups (Alexander, 2010; Bell, 1992; Blackmon, 2008; Epps, 2001; Herrnstein & Murray, 1994; Holt, 1969; Johnson, 2013; Kozol, 1991; National Center for Education Statistics, 2011; Wilson, 1993). Throughout the years, we have seen standardized tests carelessly and dangerously employed and then renormed and renamed like a psychotropic drug about to lose its sole exclusivity patent. We have seen special education turn into an idea to help students with reduced capabilities to the premiere pipeline that lead students from school to prison as efficient.

What real options do the most disadvantaged of our society have? Most of these precious souls are left with a Hobson Choice (Obiakor & Gibson, 2016; Smith, 2015). This is the quintessential take it or leave it ultimatum coined after Thomas Hobson, a livery stable owner, who refused to change the order of his horses regardless of the size or need of the customer. The customer basically had to be lucky to get the perfect horse that fit them—if not they were out of luck. But, our schools shouldn't be like this; in fact, it goes against the very spirit that was the impetus to create the EHA. Due to its continued failed results, many choose to remove themselves from a system that can be emotionally traumatic for a student. In the documentary *Nas*, Nasir Jones' father encouraged his two sons to drop out of school from the New York Public School system. Nas' mother and others were furious at the advice, as they understood the serious ramifications of a man from African ancestry with no formal education in America. The advice was not as reckless as it initially appeared. Mr. Jones tells his sons to drop out of school; but, encouraged them to read and learn material that built and strengthened self-knowledge and self-esteem. He wanted them to leave before the school killed their dreams, efficacy, esteem, and thirst for knowledge. What then can we do to identify and assess our children? This chapter answers this question.

IDENTIFYING YOUNG CHILDREN

Special education measurably began in earnest when laws were passed to respond to the needs of children and youth with exceptionalities. As indicated, the most recent change to the law was in 2004 as IDEIA. The goal and right of IDEIA, as well as its predecessors, is to provide free and appropriate public education (FAPE) for eligible children and youth ages 3–21. According to the National Center for Statistics (2017), "Eligible children are those identified by a team of professionals as having a disability that adversely affects academic performance and as being in need of special education and related services" (p. 2). Central to the question of eligibility is the identification of tools and mechanisms which determine who qualifies for special education. What then are the critical issues that are tied to the identification of students? This section responds to this question.

Benefits of Special Education

The benefits of special education are vast. It is readily seen in the states special education procedural safeguards. In particular, students who qualify have a right to a FAPE and those that qualify, regardless of the nature or severity of the disability, must be provided an "appropriate" education designed to meet their individual needs in the LRE. This helps to assure that a student is not discriminated against and instruction is tailored at his/her child's level of attainment. Another benefit of special education is that the local education agency (LEA) is required to make multiple attempts to involve parents and keep them informed and solicit parent participation throughout the IEP process. For example, parents/guardians are required to receive prior written notice of a referral, as well as give parental consent for initial evaluation and upon qualifying placement. Parent involvement is encouraged throughout the process. The procedural safeguards also outline the steps parents should take to file a complaint. These safeguards help to keep parents/guardians involved and provide a remedy for disagreements.

Eligibility Requirements

Eligibility speaks to how we qualify children for special education. Each state has developed a list of qualifiers for each of the 13 federally recognized disability categories, including autism, developmental disability, specific learning disability, intellectual impairment, emotional and/or behavioral disability, intellectual disability, speech and language disability, deaf-blind, visual impairment, hearing impairment, orthopedic or physical impairment, other health impaired (including attention deficit disorder), and multiple exceptionalities and traumatic brain injury.

One disability area that has received considerable attention around qualification has been *specific learning disability*. Many states recently began using the response to intervention (RTI) model to help determine eligibility. Prior to RTI, the discrepancy model was used for determination purposes.

Since 1977, states were required to use a "discrepancy" model for determining whether a child would qualify for a learning disability. This model assessed whether a significant discrepancy existed between one's measured level of achievement and intellectual functioning in one or more of the following areas: (a) oral expression, (b) basic reading skill, (c) reading comprehension, and (d) mathematical calculation or mathematical reasoning. A significant discrepancy was thought to exist if a child's achievement in one of the aforementioned areas falls at or below a certain percentage of a child's expected achievement level. Criticism levied at the discrepancy model cites concerns for the long period of time a student must wait in order to demonstrate a significant discrepancy. Anderson-Irish (2013) referred to this as the "wait to fail" model. In many instances, the IEP team had to wait until the child failed to provide additional services. Specifically, the conclusion of the initial evaluation for a learning disability results in a student not qualifying because he/she is not low enough academically. These students were often referred to as "grey area kids." Their skills were low but not quite low enough to meet the threshold of a "significant discrepancy" to qualify. Often, it is not until 3 years later upon re-referral where the child finally became "low enough" for the team to provide additional resources and services. The aforementioned model is no longer operational.

The current reauthorization of IDEIA in 2004 regulated that states are no longer required to use the discrepancy between intellectual ability and achievement. A second regulation associated with the reauthorization was the option of using a process based on a child's response to a scientific researched based intervention (SRBI). Anderson-Irish (2013) indicated that the RTI model was developed to replace the discrepancy model and noted that "the RTI model should be seen as a pre-referral intervention strategy that will successfully identify strategies that meet the child's specific academic needs" (p. 68). So, essentially prior to a child being referred, the regular education teacher should initiate a SRBI, coupled with regular progress monitoring, to see whether adequate gains are being made.

ASSESSING STUDENTS

Assessment is the engine behind special education placement and provision of instruction. Without assessment, no placement or program provision is authentic. Below are assessment-related activities that are helpful in knowing where students have been, where they are, and where they are going.

Observations

The assessment tools used in a special education evaluation varies from case to case. The instrument selected by individual IEP team members depend on the referral concerns and the existence of current records. For instance, if the referral source expressed concerns for behavior team members might include observations, interviews and rating scales. An effective school psychologist will make multiple observations, in structured and unstructured settings at different times of the day. Observations can include (a) a time sampling, (b) event recording, (c) narrative recording, or (d) an A-B-C recording which allows for the examination of antecedents, behavior and consequences for the referred behavior. The type of recording selected depends on the behavior in question and what one hopes to capture.

Interviews and Rating Scales

Gathering accurate information is paramount to a complete assessment. Therefore, at the school level, it is important to interview several of the child's teachers. Typically, at least one academic teacher in a core subject area such as English or mathematics and an elective teacher (e.g., art). A school psychologist begins with an unstructured interview format that is followed by direct questions that are intended to fill in the gaps and develop a fuller picture of the child. The school psychologist assesses how the student learns and functions academically and behaviorally. This provides some insight into possible impediments to acquire and retain information. School psychologists listen to what the teacher has done to help determine which measures will be most effective. Lastly, the school psychologist compares the student's level compared to students that are matched at both their chronological and mental ages. Next, the parent and the student are interviewed. The parent interview time is used to gather historical information regarding the child's birth, any medical conditions, medication prescriptions, exposure to trauma, and any changes in the family dynamics. Psychologists are also interested in how the child functions outside of school—in the home and community. What are their interaction like with siblings, age-matched relatives, and children in the neighborhood? Key to parents' interview is the assessment of the child's current level. In particular, do they have any concerns? And, if so, when did they begin? In the interview with the child, did the psychologists want to understand how the child's assessment or perspective of the current situation. Do they recognize a problem or a concern and, if so, are they motivated to make a change?

Rating scales are very helpful in the assessment process. There is a wide range of rating scales to choose from such as: (a) the Behavior Assessment Scale for Children, 3rd edition, (b) Conners, (c) Child Behavior Checklist, and (d) Achenbach System. The scale you choose, as with any tool, depends on the referral concern. Common to many rating scales is the presence of subscales that asses concerns such as inattention, hyperactivity, learning problems, depression, anxiety, social concerns, and oppositional behavior. These tools also typically have a form dedicated to the parent, teacher, and student. This helps to see the child from each of the informant's vantage point. The scales often employ a Likert scale type response format, which runs the continuum of *strongly agree* (1) to *strongly disagree* (5).

Intellectual Assessment

When a student's cognitive functioning is central to the referral, there are many instruments that could be used such as: (a) the Wechsler Intelligence Scale for Children, (b) Stanford Binet, (c) Kaufman Assessment Battery, (d) Differential Abilities Scale, (e) Cognitive Assessment Scale, (f) Bayley Scale of Infant and Child Development, and (g) the Woodcock-Johnson Tests of Cognitive Abilities. No matter the instrument, cognitive tests typically involve measures to varying degrees of language development, memory, fluid reasoning, visual-spatial ability, auditory ability, and mathematics. It is important to note that results from an IQ test is a snapshot of the child's current level.

Traditional Therapeutic Techniques

School psychologists employ a range of traditional therapeutic modalities such as cognitive behavioral therapy (CBT), rational emotive behavioral therapy (REBT), family systems therapy, brief solution focused therapy, and Rogerian. The interventions selected depend in part on the student, the psychologist's theoretical orientation, and the time frame the psychologist must work with the student. In the past, a variety of interventions took prominence such as, play therapy, art therapy, pet therapy, token economy, paradoxical techniques, and self-help interventions. In more recent years, meditation, mindfulness and yoga has gained greater emphasis. The shift towards mindfulness and meditation appears to be due impart to the recognition that many urban youths are experiencing increasing levels of traumatic events. For example, Jenkin, Wang, and Turner's (2009), study involved 403 early adolescent African American youth and found that 93% of the students reported seeing violence, 34% reported seeing someone shot by a gun, 13% saw someone killed, and 43% reported witnessing acts of violence by adults in their home within the last year. As such, it appears that schools have responded with a shift towards mindfulness. Mindfulness is heralded (e.g., Follette, 2016; Follette, Palm, & Pearson, 2006) as being an effective technique for reducing stress. According to Vujanovic, Niles, Pietrefesa, Schmertz, & Potter (2013), "Mindfulness practice may increase an individual's ability to attend to thoughts and emotions as they arise and to tolerate distressing internal experience by observing their transient nature" (p. 25). The use of mindfulness in the school is best illustrated in the following case study.

THE CASE OF JOHNATHAN

Johnathan was a 16-year-old African American youth, enrolled in the 10th grade. He was referred for special education with a suspected need in the area of emotional behavioral disorder. In the past 3 years, he had little contact with either biological parent and within an 8-month period he was residing in his second group home. At the current group home, concerns were reported for hoarding food, not completing chores, and being in constant conflict with other residents. In the school setting, a review of incident referrals, detailed concerns for chronic disruption, failure to follow school rules, theft, assault, and fighting. A classroom teacher described Johnathan, academically, as being capable of performing at grade level. However, she noted that his attendance and behavior compromised his success. In particular, he was often off-task, rarely completed projects, and was easily "setoff." Another teacher reported similar academic skills and noted that he can "go from 0–60 with little known provocation." During the evaluation, Johnathan vividly detailed traumatic events from as early as the third grade. These events ranged from physical abuse and neglect to witnessing a close friend being shot and killed. However, cumulative records indicated that the trauma actually began at 8 months of age when he was physically abused by his mother's boyfriend. On qualifying for special education services the IEP team recommended mandated services by the school psychologist.

Regarding the case above, a great deal of time was spent building trust and fostering a safe nonjudgmental environment. As time went on, Johnathan began to explore the origins of his emotions. He was able to identify the various traumas that he thought contributed to his explosiveness. Armed with his new-found realizations, the focus moved more towards meditation and mindfulness. Johnathan was introduced to guided imagery and progressive muscle relaxation. He was given biofeedback dots (skin thermometers) to monitor his stress level. These skin thermometers are sensitive to the temperature of the hand. The warmer the hands the greater the state of relaxation. For instance, hand temperatures around 95°F turned the skin thermometer dark blue to violet. An elevated level of tension was associated with a hand temperature of 89°F and the skin thermometer was black in color. Johnathan was also provided a calendar to chart his stress level and look for any trends of when he was most stressed. This helped Johnathan to realize that he could positively influence and control his mood as well as be more aware of situations that affected his mood. It was also important that Johnathan was taught the fundamentals of both formal and informal, mindfulness practices. He learned how to center his "self" and pay attention without judgment to his inner and outer experiences. These mindfulness activities can be done anywhere (e.g., home, classroom, or bus) in a standing or sitting position in as little as 20 seconds. As part of his formal mindful practices, he was also introduced to a Tibetan singing bowl, mind jar, and a breathing ball. It was posited that if Johnathan could recognize how he was feeling he could proactively take charge and utilize a relaxation exercise or breathing technique to reduce his level of stress. In the end, Johnathan could demonstrate greater control of his anger and anxiety. His incident referrals dropped from an average of six referrals per month to a little over two. When Johnathan had an episode, on average, it was shorter in duration and presented with less intensity. As a result, his grades showed steady improvement and he received the maximum number of credits by the end of the year.

OUTSIDE-THE-BOX INTERVENTIONS

One of the more difficult challenges that can occur during a special education evaluation is the realization that, despite all the resources used and intervention times the student is not eligible for services. For many parents and teachers, this outcome can easily lead to frustration and resentment towards the staff that completed the evaluation. Hopes have been laid on the possibility that if the child meets criteria of services and is found to have a need for special services, then a great weight will be lifted off everyone. Unfortunately, this is rarely the case.

THE CASE OF ALEX

Alex is an 11-year-old student who meets the criteria for special education under the classification Other Health Impairment for his attention deficit hyperactivity disorder condition. It takes a lot to complete a thorough evaluation. For example, one must administer multiple tests, conduct a multitude of observations, collect interviews from students, parents, and teachers. The results of this collaborative data determined if Alex would qualify as a student with an educational health impairment. Team members found it very easy to make this determination. From the team's observation, Alex was textbook representation of this disorder. We needed to answer two specific questions to confirm the diagnosis: (a) Does this student have an impairment? and (b) Does this impairment significantly impact educational performance? The team's first answer was easily answered in the affirmative. This was absolutely a medical impairment that could be substantially documented through the formal collection of data. The second question was not so easily answered; thus, was the genesis of a problem, sadly too often encountered by educators within the field.

Multiple sources of data have indicated that Alex is capable of sustained focused attention on material which he found an interest. The teachers who have instructional styles that are congruent with his strengths can capture his attention. Even more, these educators can prompt him to refocus and help him to maximize his instructional time in classroom settings. Despite the fact that he has low grades, often due to poor work completion, he is quite capable of understanding the lessons and as evidenced by his ability to function on the upper pyramidal elements of Bloom's taxonomy. Alex is one of many students who essentially "qualify," but have "no need." As educators, this type of student can bring multiple challenges for educators and the overall system. There is often a hope, a wish, or prayer that through the mere acquisition of special education services, this student will miraculously, through osmosis or some other divine intervention, get everything needed to be successful. Years of failure in special education reminds educators and practitioners that this is not true, but for guardians and parents who have few options and resources, the failure to receive any services, is unacceptable. After it appeared Alex would not qualify for an individualized education plan, the team decided to pursue a Section 504 accommodation plan in acknowledgment of the documented medical condition.

Accommodations Under Section 504

A possible way to level the field for students who display difficulty in traditional settings, especially those who have a physical or medical condition, is the Section 504 accommodation plan. Section 504 of the Rehabilitation Act of 1973 (P.L. 93-112) is federal legislative guidance designed to prevent discrimination in the workplace against people with disabilities. Later, it was amended to add protections for children with disabilities, in schools who receive federal funding. These plans provide accommodations that allow for equal access to education. The student must have a physical or medical condition that "substantially" affects education. Although "substantial" is an ambiguous term to encompass a variety of interpretations; multi-disciplinary teams must formally evaluate the impact of the disability to make a determinate. A Section 504 plan is to ensure the document provides legal protection for the student and the family. This plan is to guide educators and ensure the student has equal access to navigate through the educational environment to maximize the possibility for instruction in the LRE.

Strategies for Behavioral Support

The RTI strategies of tiered interventions have been the fallback solution for students who need skill development. One of the fundamental purposes of RTI is to find the right scientific research based interventions or strategies that work in development of skill deficits (Klinger & Edwards, 2006). Specifically, in the area of behavior, the highest levels of support often include functional behavioral assessments (FBA) and the use of an educational wraparound approach to problem-solving. According to Anderson, Rodrigues, and Campbell (2015), FBA can be defined as a "pre-intervention assessment conducted to develop a hypothesis about environmental variables that evoked or maintained a problem behavior" (p. 304). The FBA process provides the evaluation team a data-based sense of what drives and maintains a students' problem behaviors. This assessment provides team members with needed information to develop a behavior improvement plan (BIP) based on the hypothesized function of behavior. The goal is to find a replacement behavior that serves the same function, as a step towards complete behavior modification. The process is more often used within the world of special education, but is becoming more of recognizable advanced tier strategy for behavior challenged students who do not meet criteria for special education services.

Wraparound is known as a philosophy or strategy that provides services to students who have significant behavioral challenges; and includes the family as a part of a team approach to address the major issues (Bickman, Smith,

Lambert, & Andrade, 2003; Eber, Breen, Rose, Unizycki, & London, 2008). As part of a wraparound team, specific team members are selected based on the needs and desires of the student. Team members can be member of the community, school staff, close family members, or any individuals who are important to the student and family. The true effects of this approach are difficult to measure due to the lack of true consensus on the accepted operational definition of educational wraparound (Walker & Schutte, 2004); in addition, to the harsh realities that face students who are often referred for this service. The development of a more focused intent on how to meet the base needs of the child may run into a plethora of is deeper issues.

THE CASE OF MONICA

Specifically, reflect for a moment on the case of Monica. Monica was a kindergarten student who was initially referred for educational wraparound services because of parental refusal to comply with the school's request for an initial evaluation of a suspected emotional behavioral disability. According to the parent, her child did not experience these issues at home or in the community, so it was the responsibility of the school to address the issue in-house. Additionally, the parent expressed concern that her child was in fact gifted, and in need of a more rigorous instructional approach. The challenge for the multi-disciplinary team in this situation was to navigate the needs of the school from the perspective of the parent. Sarcastically, many members of the team snickered and ignored the possibility that Monica could be "academically gifted." However, several team members knew it was important to acknowledge the words and explore this concept. It is precisely this type of attitude that give rise to the reluctance of many parents, especially of students who are frequently disenfranchised and marginalized, to even want to engage in the initial procedure for additional services.

It is important to note that once a student is identified with specific needs, countless hours of work and meetings will follow for years. The legendary basketball coach, John Wooden, stated "we must never confuse activity with productivity" (Wooden & Carty, 2009). Sadly, many professionals fail to see the type of results in most of their students that reveal and justify their years of work. Even more sadly, students who do not qualify for services and are returned to general education classes have a similar, or worst, academic fate. If the student does not have a disability, or has met criteria but not found to be significantly educationally impacted by the disability, there is a need for a more creative approach to increase educational achievement. If the student's educational achievement delays are not related to the disability area, there is likely a need to reexamine the curriculum, instruction, and environment for learning.

Students not found eligible for special education services may still show evidence of academic skills delays which require a need for more focused intervention services. An examination of the student's strengths and challenge in combination with interaction of his/her ecological systems, on both a micro and macro level is paramount for sustained success. If the goal is to educate all students in the LRE, it is important that psychologists and related professionals engage culturally and linguistically diverse (CLD) students in the examination of traditional and non-traditional strategies to maximize success inside and outside of the classroom. The repetitive narrative among educators continues to circle around the need for more culturally responsive practices for students. More specifically, there is a push for CLD students of color to be given an environment with the appropriate curriculum and educators who can instruct it in a way to capture the entire class. Ladson-Billings (1994) asserted that effective learning conditions are created when teachers recognize the importance of culture. This change should be substantial and not merely ceremonial in nature, where the teacher changes the name from Becky to She'Quana in a word problem. Culturally relevant material should be infused into daily curriculum, as opposed to special opportunities to inject "diversity" in lessons that are outdated and irrelevant to the class. To empower students to seize their own educational opportunities is the fundamental premise behind the concept of critical pedagogy.

CONCLUSION

Assessments as we know today, have proven to be ineffective for *all* students (Johnson, 2013; Smith, 2015). This fact does not necessitate that the entire special education system should be dismantled; however, it should be reevaluated on how to use more effective assessment measures to identify students that are negatively disproportionately affected by the limitations of the current system. Psychologists and other practitioners educators have detailed how the landscape of American life has changed over the past decades with an increase in the prison industrial complex, children involved in the foster care system, systemic racism, increased poverty, and ever increased reliance on prescription medication, out of control student–teacher ratios (Alexander, 2010; Coates, 2015; Darmanin, 2003; Hatcher, 2016; Needham, Cronsoe, & Muller 2004; Perry, 2006; Schmidt & Salisbury, 2009) has a deleterious effect on the school system; and subsequently, the efficacy of reliable assessments for these students.

The current assessment system is not perfect, but we must work within it. When psychologists use current achievement and intellectual standardized tests, it is imperative that they continue to understand that (a) these assessments are snapshots of an individual; (b) these measures have a history of biasness toward CLD learners; (c) there are personal biases for the psychologist who conducts the assessment to be aware of for each assessment; (d) these assessments measure the success of each student that matriculates through their special education program. Special education was never designed to be a placement for difficult students to manage, but a *special* educational environment to help students who struggled to reach a level on par with age related peers.

Progressive psychologists will continually search for various assessments or substitutes to traditional assessments to accurately gauge their students and get them the appropriate help that will allow them to educationally elevate. These outside-the-box thinkers will help to properly assess and identify students that are too often mis-assessed and misplaced (Obiakor, Harris-Obiakor, & Smith, 2002). Assessments are the engine behind special education. Therefore, it is imperative that the process begins properly. When the initial assessments are skewed, the collected information misinforms placement, and consequently produces a fraudulent curriculum for instructors which has a continual negative spiral effect on the student who is improperly instructed. Data from the Schott report (Jackson, 2008) reveal the lasting consequences on students, families, and the American society as a whole when educational professionals continue to fail our educational constituency.

REFERENCES

Abdul-Jabbar, K., & Obstfeld, R. (2016). *Writings on the wall: Searching for new equality beyond Black and White.* New York, NY: Time Inc.

Alexander, M. (2010). *The new jim crow: Mass incarceration in the age of colorblindness.* New York, NY: The New Press.

Anderson-Irish. (2013). The over identification of minority males in middle school special education programs: Examining the RTI model. *Journal of the American Academy of Special Education Professionals,* Winter, 63–72.

Bell, D. (1992). *Faces at the bottom of the well: The permanence of racism.* New York, NY: Basic Books.

Bickman, L., Smith, C. M., Lambert, E. W., & Andrade, A. R. (2003). Evaluation of a congressionally mandated wraparound demonstration. *Journal of Child and Family Studies, 12*(2), 135–156.

Blackmon, D. A. (2008). *Slavery by another name: The re-enslavement of Black Americans from the civil war to world war II.* New York, NY: Anchor Books.

Coates, T. (2015). *Between the world and me.* New York, NY: Spiegel & Grau.

Darmanin, M. (2003). When students are failed: 'Love' as an alternative education discourse? *International Studies in Sociology of Education, (13)*2, 141–170.

Eber, L., Breen, K., Rose, J., Unizycki, R. M., & London, T. H. (2008). Wraparound as a tertiary level intervention for students with complex emotional/

behavioral needs and their families and teachers. *Teaching Exceptional Children, 40*(6), 16–22.

Epps, E. G. (2001). Race, class, social inequality, and special education: Summary comments. In C. A. Utley & F. E. Obviator (Eds.), *Special education, multicultural education, and school reform: Components of quality education for learners with disabilities* (pp. 228–236). Springfield, IL: Charles C. Thomas.

Follette, V. (2016). Rumination and mindfulness related to multiple types of trauma exposure. *Translational Issues in Psychological Science, 2*(4), 395–407.

Follette, V., Palm, K., & Pearson, A. (2006). Mindfulness and trauma: Implications for treatment. *Journal of Rational-Emotive & Cognitive-Behavioral Therapy, 24*(1), 45–61.

Hatcher, D. L. (2016). *The poverty industry: The exploitation of America's most vulnerable citizens.* New York, NY: New York University Press.

Herrnstein, R. J., & Murray, C. (1994). *The bell curve: Intelligence and class structure in American life.* New York, NY: The Free Press.

Holt, J. (1969). How children fail. In R. Gross & B. Gross (Eds.), *Radical school reform* (pp. 59–77). New York, NY: Simon & Schuster.

Jackson, J. H. (2008). *Given half of chance: The Schott 50 state report on public education and black males.* Retrieved from www.blackboyreport.org

Johnson, U. (2013). *Psycho-academic holocaust: the special education and adhd wars against Black boys.* Philadelphia, PA: Prince of Pan-Africanism.

Klinger, J. K., & Edwards, P. A. (2006). Cultural considerations with response to intervention models. *Reading Research Quarterly, 32,* 108–117.

Kozol, J. (1991). *Savage inequalities: Children in American schools.* New York, NY: Crown.

Ladson-Billings, G. (1994). *The dream keepers: Successful teachers of African-American children.* San Francisco, CA: Jossey-Baas.

National Center for Education Statistics. (2017). The condition of education 2017. Children and Youth with Disabilities. Chapter: 2: Participation in Education Section: Elementary/Secondary. Retrieved from https://nces.ed.gov/programs/coe/pdf/Indicator_CGG/coe_cgg_2017_05.pdf

Needham, B. L., Cronsoe, R., & Muller, C. (2004). Academic failure in secondary school: The Inter-related role of health problems and educational context. *Social Problems, 51*(4), 569–586.

Obiakor, F. E., & Gibson, L. (2016). Reversing the use of Hobson's Choice: Culturally relevant assessment and treatment practices for culturally and linguistically diverse learners with problem behaviors. *The Journal of the International Association of Special Education, 16*(1) 77–88.

Obiakor, F. E., Harris-Obiakor, P., & Smith, R. (2002). The comprehensive support model for all learners: Conceptualizations and meaning. In F. E. Obiakor, P. A. Grant, & E. A. Dooley (Eds.), *Educating all learners* (pp. 3–17). Springfield, IL: Charles C. Thomas.

Rose, D. H. & Meyer, A. (Eds.). (2006). *A practical reader in universal design for learning.* Cambridge: MA. Harvard Education Press.

Sailor, W. (2017). Equity as a basis for inclusive educational systems change. *Australasian Journal of Special Education, 41*(1), 1–17.

Schmidt III, H., & Salsbury III, R. E. (2009). Fitting treatment to context: Washington State's integrated treatment model for youth involved in juvenile justice. *Emotional and Behavioral Disorders in Youth, 9*(2), 31–38.

Smith, R. (2015). The school system: Old school, new school, true school. *The Milwaukee Community Journal, 39*(40), 1, 8.

Smith, R., & Sapp, M. (2005). Insights into educational psychology: What urban school practitioners must know. In F. E. Obiakor & F. D. Beachum (Eds.), *Urban education for the 21st century: Research, issues, and perspectives* (pp. 100–113). Springfield, IL: Charles C. Thomas.

United States Department of Education. (2010). *Thirty-five years of progress in educating children with disabilities through idea.* Retrieved from http://www.ed.gov/about/offices/list/osers/reports.html

Utley, C. A., & Obiakor, F. E. (2001). Multicultural education and special education: Infusion for better schooling. In C. A. Utley & F. E. Obiakor (Eds.), *Special education, multicultural education, and school Reform: Components of quality education for learners with disabilities* (pp. 3–29). Springfield, IL: Charles C. Thomas.

Vujanovic, A., Niles, B., Pietrefesa, A., Schmertz, S., & Potter, C. (2013). Mindfulness in the treatment of posttraumatic stress disorder among military veterans. *Spirituality in Clinical Practice, 1*(S), 15–25. http://dx.doi.org/10.1037/2326-4500.1.S.15

Walker, J. S., & Schutte, K. M. (2004). Practice and process in wraparound teamwork. *Journal of Emotional and Behavioral Disorders, 12*, 182–192.

Wilson, A. (1993). *The falsification of Afrikan consciousness: Eurocentric history, psychiatry and the politics of white supremacy.* New York, NY: Afrikan World InfoSystems.

CHAPTER 3

PLACEMENT OF YOUNG STUDENTS WITH EXCEPTIONALITIES

To Include or Not to Include

Lenwood Gibson Jr.

The wealth of any nation exists within the strength and education of its young children. An investment in the high-quality education of students, is an investment in the future security and prosperity of the country and the entire global community. The United States of America professes to provide this high-quality education of all of the children who attend its public-school systems. This includes students from all racial, ethnic, religious, and socioeconomic backgrounds, and also includes students who have been identified as having exceptional learning needs (ELNs).

It is common knowledge that the most vulnerable students deserve the same rights and education as all other students. Unfortunately, for much of the modern educational era, many students in need of a highest-quality education receive services that are subpar (Guo, Sawyer, Justice, & Kaderavek, 2013; Pelatti, Dynia, Logan, Justice, & Kaderavek, 2016). Although

Educating Young Children With and Without Exceptionalities, pages 31–47
Copyright © 2019 by Information Age Publishing

the causes of such educational disparity are multifaceted, some fault is in part due to the educational environment in which students with ELN are educated. The purpose of this chapter is to provide an overview of the placement process of young students. In addition, it focuses on how the potential for young children with exceptionalities can be maximized in all settings.

OVERVIEW OF EXCEPTIONALITIES

When discussing students with exceptionalities, it is helpful to understand how their learning needs are different from their non-disabled peers. According to the Individuals With Disabilities Education Improvement Act (IDEIA, 2004), there are 13 distinct categories for students with exceptionalities. Students in each of these categories have been assessed and identified as having a disability (or multiple disabilities) that require(s) an individualized educational plan (IEP) to provide accommodations, modifications, and supports in the classroom environment. The goal of all of these supports is to help students with disabilities gain access to the academic, social, and behavioral experiences needed to be successful in school and in life.

Although the 13 classifications subsume many students within school systems nationwide, there are still students who have ELNs that do not fall into any of these classifications. These may include students from culturally and linguistically diverse (CLD) backgrounds, English language learners, students "at risk" for academic failure, homeless students, and students who live near or below the poverty line. Although not all students from these groups have ELN, many are faced with additional challenges when it comes to learning and socializing in school settings (Chouari, 2016; Chu, 2011; Lee, Zhang, & Schwartz, 2006). Often times, these students are in need of supports to be successful but can go underserved (Bettini, Cumming, Merrill, Brunsting, & Liaupsin, 2017; Cramer, 2015). As a result their learning and social outcomes wane in comparison to their peers (Chu, 2011).

Students with ELN, within and across categories, often lack a wide range of skills needed to be successful in the typical classroom environment (i.e., general education). Areas of impact include academic performance, social and behavioral skills, and functional life skills. Depending on the specific skill level of individual students, instructional programs and strategies can be quite intensive. Research on best practices for students with ELN supports the early identification and teaching of skills across specified domains (Sadler & Sugai, 2009). Central to the focus on educating young learners is the need to assess skills and implement strategies to help abate the need for life-long, intensive services (Anderson & Phillips, 2017; Macy, Marks, & Towle, 2014; Partanen & Siegel, 2014). However, the intensity and quality of strategy implementation often depends on factors related to resources, teacher expertise, and student placements. Additional factors to be considered are related to the types and accuracy of the assessment procedures. The varying nature and fidelity of the assessment process can dictate outcome results and affect critical aspects of decision-making such as when/where a student is placed, level of services provided, and allocation of resources. Needless to say, students with identified ELN and those at risk, are greatly impacted by what types of educational services they receive and where and how those services are delivered.

PLACEMENT DECISIONS

A mainstay of IDEIA is that students with disabilities need to be educated in the least restrictive environment (LRE) possible for success. Typically, students identified as having a disability receive special education services that are supplemental to what their counterparts receive. These services can be delivered in several different educational settings. First, some students with ELN are placed in the typical classroom environments that use inclusion or co-teaching models. Alternatively, other students with ELN are educated in more secluded environments like self-contained classrooms. Students who exhibit the most challenging needs, are sometimes placed in specialized schools that provide very intensive services. Although locations and levels of services can be well defined by individual school systems, the placement process for deciding where individual students are educated can be complicated and may be subject to change on a year-to-year basis.

Placement decisions are largely the responsibility of the IEP teams. These teams are typically comprised of school personnel such as the special education teacher, service providers (e.g., speech-language pathologist, school psychologist, etc.), and school administration. Parents and/or guardians also make up a critical part of the team and should have considerable say on where their child is educated. Although that is not always the case, the parents are supposed to be the head of the team and central to the decision-making process. This is especially critical for young students because once they are placed in a specific educational setting (e.g., a self-contained classroom), it may be difficult to move them to less restrictive settings as they get older and/or when their skills improve. This is particularly true for students with low-incidence (i.e., severe) disabilities (Kurth, Morningstar, & Kozleski, 2014).

Identification and Referrals

Placement decisions are based on several factors that involve a multi-faceted approach to making a recommendation. These factors included: assessments and their results, professional opinions, resources, and parental advocacy. However, prior to placement decisions and recommendations being made, it is important to understand how young students are initially identified as possibly needing special education services. The identification and referral process are key factors when addressing the needs of young students. In addition, identifying young children who at risk for or have disabilities is the top priority for early childhood education professionals (Croft, 2010; Pool & Hourcade, 2011). Part C of IDEIA focuses on educational services for children from birth through 2 years old. Programs that are funded through Part C of IDEIA, center around early intervention service (EIS) and include provisions to identify young children who may be eligible for these services. One provision in the regulations requires states to implement and utilize a comprehensive "child find" system as part of a pre-referral process.

Child Find

The intent of the child find system is to have active measures in place to identify infants and toddlers who are suspected of having developmental disabilities or are at-risk for difficulties. Once identified, these young children and their families can receive EIS through their local education and/or health service agencies. The success of the child find system is predicated on the awareness to actively look for and identifying young children who may be in need of services. Professionals from the medical, social service, and educational fields (e.g., daycare providers, birth–2 teachers) are tasked with identifying children who may have developmental disabilities. If a child is suspected of having or being at risk for a developmental disability, professionals are required to make a formal referral within 7 days of identification. In addition to service providers who come into contact with young children, parents are encouraged to refer their child for services if they suspect that something is not right.

Screening and Assessments

After a formal referral is made by service professionals or parents, the identified child is screened to determine if he/she does in fact have a developmental disability. Per the regulations stipulated in Part C of IDEIA, screenings are required to be completed no later than 45 days after a formal referral is made. As part of this initial screening, the lead agency or EIS provider must obtain parental consent to conduct a multi-disciplinary evaluation to determine if the child does have a developmental disability.

Furthermore, the results of the evaluation are also used to identify specific areas in which services are most needed. Ongoing assessments are used to determine progress made toward goals and objectives outlined in an individual family service plan (IFSP). Clearly, all initial and ongoing assessments must be conducted by qualified professionals with training and experience in specific disciplines (e.g., speech and language pathology, early childhood special education, etc.). Assessments must be completed in a non-biased manner and include safeguards to account for the culturally and/or linguistically diversity of the child and family of concern. This may include conducting evaluations and assessments in the native language of the family. This provision is in place to ensure that the results of all assessments are a true indicator of an actual delay, rather than the issues surrounding language barriers.

SCHOOL-AGED STUDENTS

Although all states should have child find programs and are mandated to promote active awareness and comprehensive measure to identify very young children, there are still children who enter school with unidentified disabilities. Once a child is enrolled in the public school system, it becomes the responsibility of classroom teachers and other school-based professional to assess the needs of their students. Students who were not identified as having a disability prior to starting school, will likely be placed in general education classrooms. However, these students may quickly start to struggle within this environment; academically, socially, or both. In all cases, students need to be systematically evaluated to determine the cause and level of their needs. Schools use a variety of different strategies to evaluate the needs of young students. Many schools use standardized measures to determine how students compare to their peer group. These assessments can be conducted across academic and social domains. For example, standardized assessments like the Woodcock-Johnson IV Test of Achievement (WJ IV ACH; Schrank, Mather, & McGrew, 2014) are designed to measure math and reading skills. Whereas tools such as the Vineland Adaptive Behavior Scale (Vineland-II; Sparrow, Cicchetti, & Balla, 2005) assess socialization and behavioral skills. Another means of identifying students who may have an unidentified disability is through the use of curriculum-based measures (CBM) and progress monitoring. The Response to Intervention (RTI) is widely used to determine how students are performing within the academic curriculum (Mellard, Stern, & Woods, 2011; Sharp, Sanders, Noltemeyer, Hoffman, & Boone, 2016).

Observational Consideration

Prior to any formal assessments or referral for services, students are observed during the school day by their teachers. Classroom teachers and other staff get to see the way their students interact with classroom materials, how they engage with academic and pre-academic learning tasks, and how they socialize with their peers. Many indicators of how well a student will perform in the long term can be determined via direct observation. Students who have difficulties adjusting to classroom routines or understanding basic concepts can be red-flagged for further observation. Teachers and practitioners should be sure to keep a journal and take observational notes on young learners. This does not mean that every student that is a bit slow to adjust has a disability or in need of additional services, but that teachers should continue to observe their performance and follow up accordingly. Even the most well-intentioned professional can be subjective to his/her own biases when observing students from different cultural backgrounds. Students from CLD backgrounds may behave or interact with peers in ways that are different from their larger peer group. If these behaviors or interactions are in contrast to the cultural expectations of the observer (i.e., the teacher), these students can be falsely identified as having difficulties (Banks & Obiakor, 2015; Gibson & Obiakor, 2018; Obiakor & Gibson, 2016). Teachers and practitioners need to take cultural differences into consideration when making decisions about referring students for further evaluation.

Standardized Assessments

As noted earlier, standardized assessment tools are frequently used to determine a student's academic, cognitive, and/or social performance. These assessments are conducted by professionals who are trained in how to administer test protocols, collect data, and interpret results. Student profiles are created to give professionals some base to compare outcomes across peer groups. Many standardized assessments are considered norm referenced, meaning that standardized scores are compared to the norm group's average score. For academic based standardized assessments, students are typically compared across grade levels and/or age ranges. For example, a first-grade student's score from a standardized assessment for reading comprehension is compared to the average score of other first graders and/or other students who are roughly the same chronological age. Standardized test scores are presented as percentiles and the results are adequate for comparison across a wide variety of academic subjects.

Standardized assessments are common place in education and are used to make decisions on whether students have ELN, placement decisions, and to monitor if any gains are made. Although educational professionals rely on these tools, they do not always provide a complete account of student performance. There are several factors that can produce results that are less than reliable. These include the (a) proficiency of the professional administering the assessment, (b) behavior of the students being tested (i.e., test anxiety), and (c) inherent nature of standardized exams that make them culturally biased. The last two points are particularly important when discussing the outcome measure of young students and students from CLD background. Young students may be apprehensive when entering into a new and unfamiliar environment. The beginning of the school year for pre-kindergarten and kindergarten students can be a traumatizing experience. This can be particularly true for young students from CLD backgrounds if their new teachers are not familiar with their cultural norms and/or do not speak their language. Although it is important to observe and assess young students very soon after they enter into school, subjecting them to assessment procedures that they have never been exposed to before can be even further upsetting. Even students who do not have language barriers may still exhibit anxiety when they are placed in "testing" situations. In order to obtain the most accurate results, test administrators should spend some time building a friendly rapport with students prior to assessments being administered.

One common reason for inaccurate results of standardized assessments is due to test biases. Test bias refers to the content of testing material in relation to the cultural background of the students taking the test. Due to the fact that our society has what is considered a "dominate" culture, much of the assessment materials used to determine performance of students is based on the standards of this culture. Culturally biased material does not take into account the differences of students from outside of the "dominate" culture that the assessments are based on. These differences may lead to students from CLD backgrounds not fully understanding or relating to the material (as opposed to not knowing the subject matter). Issues with culturally bias assessments must be taken into consideration when interpreting the results of standardized assessments for CLD students (Craig, Thompson, Washington, & Potter, 2004; Sandilos et al., 2015).

Response-to-Intervention

As an alternative (or supplement) to the reliance standardized assessment results, some schools implement a RTI to determine students' performances. Response to Intervention, is a systematic approach to assess and monitor how well individual students perform on specific skill sets that make up larger academic domains (Turse & Albrecht, 2015). For example, in order to determine the reading proficiency of young students, they would be given benchmark assessments that focused on skills such as letter recognition and letter–sound correspondence. Students who score at or below basic levels are identified as needing more intensive academic instruction and more frequent follow-up assessments to determine progress (i.e., their response to the intervention).

In the RTI model, all students are administered benchmark assessments at least three different times throughout the school year. Typically, these assessments occur at the beginning, middle, and towards the end of the year. Benchmark assessments utilize CBM that are designed to represent grade level academics (McAlenney & McCabe, 2012). Curriculum-based measures are designed to be delivered quickly and assess multiple skill sets at the same time. Students' skills are generally divided into three categories: at isk, some risk, and low risk. These categories are associated with specific benchmark scores for each academic sub-test and provide the information needed to make decisions on the intensity of academic instruction and student groupings. Typically, these students are placed in small groups and receive additional instruction in the identified skills set. Tier two students also are more closely monitored to determine if the additional instruction is effective in improving the targeted skill(s). Known as "progress monitoring," students are assessed using CBM every several weeks. It is generally thought that many students will respond favorably during tier two intervention and acquire the skills needed to return to tier one (i.e., whole class instruction). Those students who do not respond to tier two instruction and continue to struggle are moved to tier three instruction which consists of very intensive intervention (one-to-one instruction). When implemented correctly, the RTI model is fairly effective in identifying students in need of additional instruction and monitoring their progress towards becoming "low risk" in specific skills (Catts, Nielsen, Bridges, Liu, & Bontempo, 2015).

Discrepancy Model Versus RTI

Although there are several approaches in determining performance levels and service needs of students, it is a bit unclear about which approach leads to better outcomes for young students. As stated earlier, the use of standardized assessment tools provides a performance profile of a student that can be compared to established performance levels. Students who do not meet the criteria set by these levels are identified as having deficiencies in one or more areas. Depending on how far below the cut score a student's performance is, he/she can be found to have a "severe discrepancy." The severe discrepancy model (SDM) focuses on the outcomes of standardized test scores in comparison with the established norms (Peterson & Shinn,

2002). Students found to have a severe discrepancy are identified as having a learning disability and then qualify for special education services. Although the SDM is traditionally and widely used for identifying students with ELNs, it can be problematic when used with very young students. Concerns with using the SDM with young students are that it does not take into account several important factors for this population demographic. First, the nature of child development is such that some young students need more time than others to acquire specific skills. So, rather than having a true skill deficit due to a disability, some students perform poorly on an assessment because they are yet to catch up developmentally with his/her peers. Second, many young students come to school with varying degrees of background knowledge and early educational experiences. For example, students who have not been exposed to a literacy rich environment may not perform particularly well on standardized reading assessments until they are taught the needed skills in school. This might be particularly true for students from CLD backgrounds if English is not the language spoken in their homes.

As an alternative to the SDM, the use of RTI to identify "at-risk" students has become increasingly popular among school systems. The ease of implementation and readily available results provided by benchmark and progress monitoring assessments (e.g., CBM) allow for this model to be implemented with students in all grade/age ranges. The use of RTI assessments may eliminate some of the issues with the SDM by not relying on standardized procedures and percentile scores to determine performance levels. Rather, student performance is based on benchmark scores for specific academic skills. For example, the benchmark score for *letter naming* (a core reading skill) at the beginning of kindergarten is eight or more letters identified correctly in one minute. Students who score below this benchmark are considered "at risk" and therefore would receive additional academic support to improve that skill. Follow up assessments are then used to determine how effective the additional support (i.e., the intervention) is for improving each identified skill. Students who continue to struggle (i.e., not meeting benchmarks) are moved to next level of support; and if they continue to struggle may be identified as needed special education services.

Although the premise of the RTI model is to prevent special education placement by identifying and providing appropriate levels of support and instruction for young students, the model is not always successful. Some critics of RTI point out several perceived flaws. First, there is a lack of standardization in terms of what is used to conduct benchmarks and progress monitoring assessments. Although widely accepted, the use of CBM may differ from school to school making generalized outcomes difficult to determine. Another problem with RTI is that it requires the use of "evidence-based" interventions as a means of addressing the identified deficiencies in specific skills sets. This requirement alone is not the problem, in fact it is sound educational practice; however, there can be inconsistencies in ensuring that the curriculum that is being used is actually "evidence based." Even when a curriculum is truly evidence based it needs to be implemented with adequate integrity to have the desired effect. It is entirely possible that students who are identified as "at risk" are not receiving the appropriate instruction to prevent further academic failure.

Taken altogether, the use of the SDM or RTI alone may not be enough to accurately and consistently identify young students with ELN or at risk for academic failure. Some combination of these two approaches may perhaps be the most effective way to determine which students are in need of special education placements. Furthermore, the information gleaned from these assessments can provide a better picture of the specific skills that need improvement and therefore allow for a more accurate individualized education plan (IEP). Finally, the outcomes of these assessments contribute to the information needed when making placement decisions. For young students, who are just beginning their time in school, it is vital that they are placed in the academic environment that will provide them with every opportunity to be successful.

SPECIAL EDUCATION PLACEMENT SETTING

As discussed earlier in this chapter, there are different types of educational environments for young students identified as having ELN. Each of these environments have pros and cons associated with the overall outcomes for these students. As the pendulum swings back and forth when considering where to best educate young students with ELN, it is helpful to understand the benefits and drawbacks for each environment.

Inclusion Classrooms

The idea of full inclusion is one side of the debate on how to best educate students with ELN. Proponents of full inclusion argue that students with ELN benefit the most when educated alongside their typically developing peers (Kirby, 2017). The premise of full inclusion is based on advocacy for equality in education. Some people believe students with ELN learn best when they are surrounded by their peers and are provided with the same educational opportunities (Obiakor, 2001). Although this is a valid argument, the implementation of full inclusion does not always live up to the premise. Some "inclusive" environments may not have the resources needed to provide the additional learning opportunities and individualized instruction required to effectively teach students with ELN (Able, Sreckovic, Schultz, Garwood, & Sherman, 2015). In those situations, inclusive classrooms may actually cause these students to fall further behind academically and/or socially.

From a social perspective, there are many benefits when educating young students with ELN in fully inclusive classrooms. These classrooms are full of typically developing peers that serve as models for appropriate social behaviors. Research supports the use of peer modeling when trying to teach young children important social skills (Puckett, Mathur, & Zamora, 2017). By having students with ELN in the same classroom or educational environment as their peers, they can develop a better understanding of social norms and may be more open to social interactions. Moreover, typically developing peers are exposed to students with ELN on a daily basis. This allows these students to understand and value differences among their peer group. At a young age, it helps to establish strong peer advocacy and a sense of responsibility to assist others who need additional supports. Clearly, the placement of young students with ELN in fully inclusive classrooms is positive and advocated for when appropriate. However, there are circumstances in which the level of service needs exceeds the capabilities of an inclusive classroom environment. The majority of students educated in fully inclusive classrooms are classified with mild to moderate ELN and therefore are likely to benefit from the structures within these environments. However, for students with more intensive ELN, inclusive classrooms may not be able to provide the appropriate level of services required to help him/her meet educational goals. These students are likely require placement in more intensive environments.

Self-Contained Classrooms

For young students who are unable to be placed in an inclusive classroom environment, the next level of placement is a self-contained classroom. Self-contained classroom environments are afforded more resources to provide greater access to intensive instruction. One such resource is a smaller number of students and more instructional staff in the classroom. Staff to student ratios are typically expressed as the number of students to the number of staff, including the special education teacher and the teaching assistants. For example, a 12:1:2 self-contained classroom would be comprised of 12 students, 1 special education teacher, and 2 teaching assistants. Higher staffing ratio (e.g., 6:1:2 vs 12:1:2) indicates that students require more intense educational services. Self-contained classrooms are most often located within the "home school" of each student. They are largely beneficial for students with moderate to severe ELN. These students are unlikely to function independently or successfully in large, less structured classrooms. Furthermore, they often require ongoing support throughout the day to adequately access the academic curriculum. Students in self-contained classroom environments are likely to spend most of their school day in their classroom, where they receive intensive supports via individualized or small group instruction. These students are also provided with additional services such as speech and language, occupational and/or physical therapy, and behavioral support services. These services are individualized according to each student's IEP.

Although the intensive supports provided in self-contained classrooms are designed to benefit individual students, there are some pitfalls of placing young students in these environments. One of the first concerns for students in self-contained classrooms is the lack of contact and socialization with their peer group. Self-contained classrooms are essentially isolated environments away from the general school population. For professionals and advocates who are knowledgeable about the history of "special education," it can be alarming to have students no matter the circumstances, separated. For many years, special education settings provided services that were totally isolated from the general population. Moreover, the quality of instruction in these classrooms was extremely poor and did not provide the types of services to meet the needs of the students. Although there has been a great deal of reform of the past several decades, the stigma of isolated settings still persists in the modern educational era, and advocates continue to push for full inclusion.

Specialized Schools

One of the most restrictive educational placement settings is generally made for students with the most severe ELN. Typically, these students exhibit extreme behavior problems (e.g., aggressive and/or self-injury) that require very high levels of support. When students cannot be supported by the services provided within a school district, they may be placed in a specialized school setting. These settings have very high staff to student ratios, such as one-to-one staffing and provide very intensive, individualized instruction. Students in these settings can be very successful in meeting their goals and objectives, but at the cost of being in a very isolated environment. Specialized schools have similar concerns as with self-contained classrooms, in that students have virtually no access to their typically developing peer groups.

CONCERNS WITH SPECIAL EDUCATION PLACEMENT

Special educations placements can and should be beneficial for young students with ELN. As long as these students are placed in appropriate educational settings, they will receive the level and intensity of services needed to meet their educational objectives. In an ideal world, the assessment and placement process is conducted in an objective and accurate manner. However, there are several caveats that need to be considered when making placements decisions. These include (a) issues of over-identification and disproportionality, (b) students continuing in more restrictive environments longer than needed, and (c) lack of contact with nondisabled peers.

Over-Identification and Disproportionality

One of the most pressing issues with special education placement involves the over-identification of CLD students in special education. In particular, young African American males are overrepresented in special education classrooms across the country. What makes this concerning is the fact that many of the referrals for these students are made because of perceived behavioral problems (Obiakor, 2001; Obiakor & Gibson, 2016; Simmons-Reed & Cartledge, 2014). There is a great deal of research that supports the fact that young African American students do not engage in measurably more problematic behaviors or their behaviors are not more severe than other students; however, they are identified and referred for special education much more often (Vincent, Tobin, Hawken, & Frank, 2012). The problems with disproportionality were so pervasive that the reauthorization of IDEIA (2004) directly addressed it and called for the disaggregation of disciplinary referrals along racial demographics. The aim was to put safeguards in place to reduce the subjectivity of behavior referrals and to develop remedies to prevent over-identification. Despite best efforts, issues of disproportionality continue to persist in special education. This is particularly problematic when related to the second caveat of long-term special education placements.

Long-Term Placement

The need for and use of special education placements is supposed to be a limited service for many students. IDEIA requires that students with ELN be educated in the LRE possible to support success. What is also required is the periodic and systematic reevaluation of students' need for services in specific settings. Through the IEP process, student progress is reviewed on an annual basis and reevaluation of services occurs every 3 years (i.e., tri-annual evaluation). During the reassessment and reevaluation processes, decisions are made in regards to (a) continuation of services, (b) the levels and intensity of services, (c) and placements for service delivery. IEP meetings all for the IEP team to have discussions about the LRE and if there is a need to change the placement. Unfortunately, all too often, students who are placed into a special education environment rarely change placements. In fact, research indicates that once placed in special education, students with ELN are likely to remain there (Kurth et al., 2014).

Although special education placements are needed to help students with ELN achieve success in school, they should not be left to languish in these environments. For students with severe disabilities, it may be necessary for long-term placement in more restrictive environments; however, many students with ELN are not considered severe. As noted with the discussion on disproportionality, many students are referred to (and ultimately placed in) special education settings due to behavioral or mild learning difficulties. These difficulties should be addressed and remedied as soon as possible so students can be returned to less restrictive environments. This is especially true for very young students since they are more receptive to high-quality instructional and behavioral interventions. The RTI model may be more adept for preventing long-term special education placements and the downsides that come along with it.

Lack of Contact

One of the major downsides when students are placed in special education settings that do not include typically developing peers (i.e., self-contained and specialized schools) is that they do not have access to their peer group. A big advantage of having students in inclusive classroom settings is that they are exposed to peer models. There is plenty of research demonstrating that peer modeling is very effective for improving behavioral and academic skills of students with ELN (Harjusola-Webb, Hubbell, & Bedesem, 2012; Stanton-Chapman & Brown, 2015). However, when students are placed in settings without their typically developing peers, they have less opportunities to be exposed to types of skills needed to be successful. To make matters worse, students with ELN who are placed in settings with other severe disabilities may have the tendency to imitate problematic behaviors. For students who are placed in restrictive settings, every effort should be made to provide opportunities to interact with their nondisabled peers.

CONCLUSION

The assessment and placement of young students with ELN are critical processes that have major impacts on the education and lives of these students. It is important that educators and service professionals are dedicated to the accurate identification, assessment, and continued evaluation of these students. Furthermore, students should be placed in settings that will allow them to receive the best possible educational outcomes in the LRE. The careful consideration of factors such as cultural and linguistic diversity must be accounted for when making placement decisions. Ultimately, it is not necessarily a question of whether to place or not to place, but the assurance that placement decisions are based on reliable and credible evidence that the student's best interest is being served. For young students with ELN, correct placement decisions can mean the difference between success and failure in school.

REFERENCES

Able, H., Sreckovic, M. A., Schultz, T. R., Garwood, J. D., & Sherman, J. (2015). Views from the trenches: Teacher and student supports needed for full inclusion of students with ASD. *Teacher Education and Special Education, 38*(1), 44–57.

Anderson, S., & Phillips, D. (2017). Is pre-k classroom quality associated with kindergarten and middle-school academic skills? *Developmental Psychology, 53*(6), 1063–1078. doi:10.1037/dev0000312

Banks, T., & Obiakor, F. E. (2015). Culturally responsive positive behavior supports: Considerations for practice. *Journal of Education and Training Studies, 3*(2), 83–90.

Bettini, E. A., Cumming, M. M., Merrill, K. L., Brunsting, N. C., & Liaupsin, C. J. (2017). Working conditions in self-contained settings for students with emotional disturbance. *Journal of Special Education, 51*(2), 83–94. doi:10.1177/0022466916674195

Catts, H. W., Nielsen, D. C., Bridges, M. S., Liu, Y. S., & Bontempo, D. E. (2015). Early identification of reading disabilities within an RTI framework. *Journal of Learning Disabilities, 48*(3), 281–297. doi:10.1177/0022219413498115

Chouari, A. (2016). Cultural diversity and the challenges of teaching multicultural classes in the twenty-first century. *Arab World English Journal, 7*(3), 3–17.

Chu, S., (2011). Perspectives in understanding the schooling and achievement of students from culturally and linguistically diverse backgrounds. *Journal of Instructional Psychology, 38*(3), 201–209.

Craig, H. K., Thompson, C. A., Washington, J. A., & Potter, S. L. (2004). Performance of elementary-grade African American students on the gray oral reading tests. *Language, Speech, and Hearing Services in Schools, 35*(2), 141–154.

Cramer, L. (2015). Inequities of intervention among culturally and linguistically diverse students. *Penn GSE Perspectives on Urban Education, 12*(1), 1–8.

Croft, C. (2010). Talking to families of infants and toddlers about developmental delays. *YC: Young Children, 65*(1), 44–46.

Gibson, L., & Obiakor, F. E., (2018). Computer-based technology for special and multicultural education: Enhancing 21st century learning. San Diego, CA: Plural.

Guarino, C. M., Buddin, R., Pham, C., & Cho, M. (2010). Demographic factors associated with the early identification of children with special needs. *Topics in Early Childhood Special Education, 30*(3), 162–175. doi:10.1177/0271121409349273

Guo, Y., Sawyer, B. E., Justice, L. M., & Kaderavek, J. N. (2013). Quality of the literacy environment in inclusive early childhood special education classrooms. *Journal of Early Intervention, 35*(1), 40–60. doi:10.1177/1053815113500343

Harjusola-Webb, S., Hubbell, S. P., & Bedesem, P. (2012). Increasing prosocial behaviors of young children with disabilities in inclusive classrooms using a combination of peer-mediated intervention and social narratives. *Beyond Behavior, 21*(2), 29–36.

Kirby, M. (2017). Implicit assumptions in special education policy: Promoting full inclusion for students with learning disabilities. *Child & Youth Care Forum, 46*(2), 175–191.

Kurth, J. A., Morningstar, M. E., & Kozleski, E. B. (2014). The persistence of highly restrictive special education placements for students with low-incidence disabilities. *Research & Practice for Persons with Severe Disabilities, 39*(3), 227–239. doi:10.1177/1540796914555580

Lee, H., Zhang, C., & Schwartz, B. (2006). Challenges of providing culturally and linguistically appropriate services: Perspectives of early intervention professionals in a northeastern metropolitan city. *Multiple Voices for Ethnically Diverse Exceptional Learners, 9*(1), 1–11.

Macy, M., Marks, K., & Towle, A. (2014). Missed, misused, or mismanaged: Improving early detection systems to optimize child outcomes. *Topics in Early Childhood Special Education, 34*(2), 94–105. doi:10.1177/0271121414525997

McAlenney, A. L., & McCabe, P. P. (2012). Introduction to the role of curriculum-based measurement in response to intervention. *Reading Psychology, 33*(1), 1–7. doi:10.1080/02702711.2012.630599

Mellard, D. F., Stern, A., & Woods, K. (2011). RTI school-based practices and evidence-based models. *Focus on Exceptional Children, 43*(6), 1–15.

Obiakor, F. E. (2001, November). Transitional teaching and learning to improve minority student achievement in inclusive settings. *Journal of Special Education Leadership, 14*, 81–88.

Obiakor, F. E., & Gibson, L. (2016). Reversing the use of Hobson's choice: Culturally relevant assessment and treatment practices for culturally and linguistically diverse learners with problem behaviors. *Journal of the International Association of Special Education, 16*(1), 77–88.

Partanen, M., & Siegel, L. (2014). Long-term outcome of the early identification and intervention of reading disabilities. *Reading & Writing, 27*(4), 665–684. doi:10.1007/s11145-013-9472-1

Pelatti, C., Dynia, J., Logan, J., Justice, L., & Kaderavek, J. (2016). Examining quality in two preschool settings: Publicly funded early childhood education and inclusive early childhood education classrooms. *Child & Youth Care Forum, 45*(6), 829–849. doi:10.1007/s10566-016-9359-9

Peterson, K. M. H., & Shinn, M. R. (2002). Severe discrepancy models: Which best explains school identification practices for learning disabilities? *School Psychology Review, 31*(4), 459–476.

Pool, J. L., & Hourcade, J. J. (2011). Developmental screening: A review of contemporary practice. *Education and Training in Autism and Developmental Disabilities, 46*(2), 267–275.

Puckett, K., Mathur, S. R., & Zamora, R. (2017). Implementing an intervention in special education to promote social skills in an inclusive setting. *Journal of International Special Needs Education, 20*(1), 25–36. doi:10.9782/2159-4341-20.1.25

Sadler, C., & Sugai, G. (2009). Effective behavior and instructional support: A district model for early identification and prevention of reading and behavior problems. *Journal of Positive Behavior Interventions, 11*(1), 35–46. doi:10.1177/1098300708322444

Sandilos, L. E., Lewis, K., Komaroff, E., Hammer, C. S., Scarpino, S. E., Lopez, L.,. . . Goldstein, B. (2015). Analysis of bilingual children's performance on the English and Spanish versions of the Woodcock-Muñoz language survey-R (WMLS-R). *Language Assessment Quarterly, 12*(4), 386–408.

Schrank, F. A., Mather N., & McGrew K. S. (2014). *Woodcock-Johnson IV Test of Achievement.* Rolling Meadows, IL: Riverside.

Sharp, K., Sanders, K., Noltemeyer, A., Hoffman, J. L., & Boone, W. J. (2016). The relationship between RTI implementation and reading achievement: A school-level analysis. *Preventing School Failure, 60*(2), 152–160.

Simmons-Reed, E., & Cartledge, G. (2014). School discipline disproportionality: Culturally competent interventions for African American males. *Interdisciplinary Journal of Teaching and Learning, 4*(2), 95–109.

Sparrow, S. S., Cicchetti, D. V., & Balla, D. A. (2005). *Vineland Adaptive Behavior Scales, Second Edition.* Minneapolis. MN: Pearson.

Stanton-Chapman, T., & Brown, T. S. (2015). A strategy to increase the social interactions of 3-year-old children with disabilities in an inclusive classroom. *Topics in Early Childhood Special Education, 35*(1), 4–14. doi:10.1177/0271121414554210

Turse, K. A., & Albrecht, S. F. (2015). The ABCs of RTI: An introduction to the building blocks of response to intervention. *Preventing School Failure, 59*(2), 83–89. doi:10.1080/1045988X.2013.837813

Vincent, C. G., Tobin, T. J., Hawken, L. S., & Frank, J. L. (2012). Discipline referrals and access to secondary level support in elementary and middle schools: Patterns across African-American, Hispanic-American, and White students. *Education & Treatment of Children, 35*(3), 431–458. doi:10.1353/etc.2012.0018

CHAPTER 4

INNOVATIVE TEACHING METHODS FOR YOUNG CHILDREN WITH AND WITHOUT DISABILITIES

Shaunita Strozier, Cindy Head, and Stephanie Marshall

In our ever changing, fast-paced world, there is a need to provide students with an education that is real, relevant, and engaging. In order to achieve this, teachers must experiment with innovative teaching methods that are geared toward truly engaging students in the curriculum and providing them with opportunities to participate in authentic tasks. Although the goal of education has always focused on helping students to become productive members of society, students today are different from those in the past. For example, students today have access to information at their fingertips. As a result, current teaching methods must reflect societal changes, and move beyond rote memorization and "teaching to the test" of the past to providing students with real world problem solving skills. This chapter provides insight into how teachers at the elementary level can develop innovative

Educating Young Children With and Without Exceptionalities, pages 49–60
Copyright © 2019 by Information Age Publishing

49

teaching methods to teach diverse student populations—both students with and without disabilities.

When considering and developing innovative teaching methods at the elementary level, teachers must take into account the diverse needs of students in general education classrooms. Due to the *least restrictive requirements* in federal education legislation such as the Individuals With Disabilities Education Act (IDEA), inclusion of students with disabilities in general education classrooms is at an all-time high. Therefore, teachers must consider and address the unique needs of individual students, including those with disabilities, when developing content. In order for students with special needs to be successful beyond their elementary school years, they too must be provided with the same high quality innovative education. In addition, technology can be used to help ameliorate some of the unique needs of a diverse population.

INNOVATION IN EDUCATION

When one hears the word "innovation," the word new often comes to mind, and according to Webster's dictionary, innovation is defined as beginning something new. In education and specifically educational teaching strategies, this can be further refined as a new idea, device, or method of teaching. Usually, when teachers hear the word innovation, the use of technology automatically comes to mind. Although innovation in education often utilizes technology to improve student achievement, the term "innovation" can also be applied to a concept that is basically original but has been enhanced by an innovative idea or component which adds to the original concept and results in greater effectiveness. In other words, innovation in education and empirically-based strategies (most of which are not considered innovative) that are required by federal legislation should not be considered mutually exclusive. With an emphasis on the use of evidence-based practices (practices not likely to be considered innovative), teachers can still implement innovative methods while simultaneously utilizing evidence-based strategies. Although an in-depth discussion of the use of evidence-based teaching methods is beyond the scope of this chapter, a brief example is provided.

Direct instruction (DI) methods developed by Engelmann and colleagues in the 1960s and 1970s is one example of an evidence-based practice that has an abundance of research to support its effectiveness. The effectiveness of DI has been shown to be effective for students from low socioeconomic backgrounds (Head, Flores, & Shippen, 2018; Torgensen et al., 2001), students at risk for academic failure (Carlson & Francis, 2002; Fredrick, Keel, & Neel, 2002; Shippen, Houchins, Steventon, & Sartor, 2005), students with learning disabilities (Swanson, 1998; Torgesen et al., 2001), students with limited English proficiency (Carlson & Francis, 2002), and students with cognitive deficits (Bradford et al., 2006; Flores, Shippen, Alberto, & Crowe, 2004). Given the evidence regarding the effectiveness of programs such as DI, elementary teachers can supplement evidence-based teaching methods to create lessons that are even more engaging for students. A couple of examples would be including gaming components to improve fluency in basic skills or adding internet-based platforms that provide immediate feedback to students to enhance mastery of skills. Regardless of the type of enhancements utilized, it is imperative that teachers continually seek ways to improve instructional delivery. As a result of these improvements and addition of innovative teaching methods, teachers can ensure improved student engagement and academic outcomes for all children. In addition, new technologies have promising ways of helping students with special needs access and participate in the general curriculum. As a result of the use of technology and increased innovative teaching methods, teachers can address complacency, passivity, and stagnation within their own classrooms and seek higher levels of success for their students. Therefore, barriers to implementing innovative teaching methods and ways in which teachers can improve upon current teaching strategies are discussed below.

As with any change, innovation in education is likely to be met with resistance by at least some. When considering innovation in education, teachers and administrators should consider common barriers that they might possibly encounter when encouraging innovation in teaching methods and strategies. One such barrier is lack of teacher buy in. Lack of buy in can be a result of various factors, but teachers today often have more and more demands placed upon them. In order to maximize teacher buy in, administrators should take into consideration factors likely to impact the likelihood of teacher buy in. For example, if a teacher is drowning in paperwork and other requirements placed upon them by administration, creating and implementing innovative teaching methods and strategies will be challenging and/or impossible. Another challenge to creating and implementing innovative teaching methods and strategies is the requirement that teachers use required programs and/or curricula, as some districts may require teachers to use and follow prescribed programs. Homogenizing curricular materials and teaching strategies stifles and stunts innovation. In addition, adding programs and curricula increase the long list of tasks that teachers are already required to do. As a result, these programs are not likely to be considered innovative; but, teachers can build upon and/or supplement required programs/curricula to make them innovative.

Perhaps one of the biggest challenges to increasing and improving innovation in education relates to the school climate. In order for innovation to occur, teachers must be provided with an environment where innovation is a priority and effective teaching methods and strategies are implemented. Often times, schools pay lip service to innovation but are lacking in execution. Also, overly rigid professional learning communities, unnecessary faculty meetings, mundane professional developments are examples of commonly found practices in elementary schools that tend to stifle innovation. In order to address these issues and increase innovation, teachers must be provided with support. The following sections provide administrators with a few, in-depth examples of innovative teaching methods and strategies that might be implemented to increase engagement and academic outcomes for with students with and without disabilities.

THEORETICAL FOUNDATIONS

Prior to discussing innovative teaching methods designed for young children with and without disabilities, it is essential to examine the theoretical foundations on which these methods, and all teaching methods, should be based. This theory, which could be considered a recent innovation itself, is growth mindset. The growth mindset, described by Carol Dweck in her 2006 book *Mindset: The New Psychology of Success*, describes a continuum of beliefs that individuals possess in regard to the origin of ability. On one end of the continuum, is the "fixed mindset," which is the belief individuals are born with (or without) innate ability or IQ and that there is not much that an individual can do about it. On the other end of the continuum is the growth mindset, in which individuals believe hard work and training can lead to improved intelligence. The differences in the two theories are best described by Dweck in a 2012 interview with James Morehead:

> In a fixed mindset students believe their basic abilities, their intelligence, their talents, are just fixed traits. They have a certain amount and that's that, and then their goal becomes to look smart all the time and never look dumb. In a growth mindset students understand that their talents and abilities can be developed through effort, good teaching and persistence. They don't necessarily think everyone's the same or anyone can be Einstein, but they believe everyone can get smarter if they work at it. (Morehead, 2015)

One important difference between the two mindsets, is the way that individuals cope with failure. In the fixed mindset, individuals avoid failure as it is viewed as lack of necessary skills and abilities; however, individuals who have a growth mindset are more likely to persist when confronted with failure, as failures are viewed as opportunities to grow given that they invest appropriate effort. These delineations are important for teachers to understand, as positive and encouraging interactions can help students to develop and/or reshape individual mindsets (Aldhous, 2008). As a teacher, it is important to consider how to develop growth mindsets in children.

When considering how to shape growth mindsets in children, it is important to examine the role of teacher-student interactions (specifically praise) in doing so. Research has demonstrated that the use of praise has differential effects. For example, praising achievement or inherent ability has been shown to promote a fixed mindset because the child becomes focused on the outcome; whereas praising strategies and effort promotes a growth mindset as the child becomes focused on the process (Gunderson, Gripshover, Romero, & Dweck, 2013; Mueller & Dweck, 1998). According the Dweck (2015), praising effort alone is not sufficient, as children often receive empty praise for just trying. This can result in creating students who are "slaves of praise" rather than creating students who embrace challenges. If children are not seeing results after a great deal of effort, teachers should focus students' attention on strategies that have previously been tried as well as strategies that have not yet been tried. Students should also seek input from others. In doing so, teachers can help students develop a love for the challenge of learning. It is essential that teachers understand the significance of the fixed versus growth mindset because fixed mindsets are related to decreasing academic performance over time whereas growth mindsets are associated with academic improvement (Blackwell, Trzesniewski, & Dweck, 2007; Good, Aronson, & Inzlicht, 2003). Furthermore, research has demonstrated that children's mindsets can be changed through intervention (Blackwell et al., 2007; Kamins & Dweck, 1999). In addition, growth mindset orientations have been shown to be useful in (a) intervention strategies with at-risk students, (b) dispelling negative stereotypes in education held by teachers and students, (c) understanding the impacts of self-theories on resilience, and (d) understanding how process praise can foster a growth mindset and positively impact students' motivation levels.

When pursuing the growth mindset, teachers should also consider strategies that promote empowerment and flexibility within his/her classroom environment (Blackwell et al., 2007). First, teachers should have developed personal growth mindsets for themselves. As an educator, teacher presence in the classroom should serve as a model and demonstrate a motivation for students to learn and use efforts within different academic and social activities. To ensure these efforts happen, teachers should give feedback that is likely to increase expected classroom behaviors. Administering praise at an adequate amount helps students with whatever processes that they have engaged in as well help them develop a growth potential (Dweck, 2006). Teachers also must remember that the praise that is given must be specific in its delivery. For example, telling a student that he/she has done a good job can be confusing and may reinforce an unwanted behavior. However, telling a student that he/she has done an excellent good job following the order of operations to complete problems on math homework allows the praise to be specifically defined. The use of specific praise is most effective when the focus is on the use of the learning strategy and the behaviors expected to do well on a task. In addition, Dweck (2006) suggested that when correcting a student's abilities, teachers should incorporate the word "yet." The word "yet" or "not yet" gives children a greater chance to experience confidence and provide a path to greater persistence, as students begin to believe that unmastered skills are attainable. Adding reinforcing words to praise leads students into mastering a growth mindset. Learning to accomplish small tasks creates a sense of accomplishment and pride in children. This process leads to curiosity, independence, and persistence.

Taking advantage of mistakes is another strategy for teachers to utilize when prompting the use of a growth mindset. Making mistakes and admitting failures are important aspects of the learning process. When students experience letdowns during the learning process, it provides short- and long-term benefits. The mistakes that students experience can be turned into learning success and mastery. Dweck (2006) explained that teachers should praise students for their efforts, but not just efforts alone. Teachers should provide additional information to help students problem-solve and become of aware of individual flaws while approaching new strategies and/or tasks. At times, teachers may have difficulty with supporting students who experience failure, but it is necessary to help the learning process progress. The final strategy that assists in encouraging a growth mindset is allowing students to experience failure. It is often not a good idea for teachers to solve problems for their students. Although it may seem easier because it prevents unwanted behavior, students miss out on the learning process (Blackwell et al., 2007). Instead, teachers should allow students to explore and fail as the process of trial and error is a way for children to learn and make discoveries about their environments and themselves. Learning from failures allows for students to become independent thinkers as well as persons who can cope with life and its challenges (Lahey, 2015). An innovative teaching method that allows for students to use problem-solving skills and also allows students to reflect on incorrect responses is a method known as problem-based learning.

PROBLEM-BASED LEARNING

Problem-based learning (PBL) is a specific innovative teaching strategy that is aligned with growth mindset. Not to be confused with project based learning, PBL is one alternative to traditional teaching methods and has gained popularity in the past couple of decades. Problem-based learning is a student centered instructional method in which students work collaboratively to solve open-ended, real world problem(s) that do not have a single correct answer. In PBL, students engage in self-directed learning to identify what they need to learn in order to solve the problem as students apply new knowledge to the problem and reflect on what they have learned. During this process, the teacher acts as facilitator. This method of teaching is in direct contrast with traditional methods of teaching which usually consist of direct instruction of facts and concepts. Although direct instruction of basic skills is an empirically based strategy for the teaching of reading, mathematics, writing, teachers must utilize various methodologies in order to maximize student interest and engagement in curricula. Problem-based learning is an alternative to traditional approaches and provides an innovative pedagogy that some view as "the most innovative pedagogical method ever implemented in education" (Hung, Jonassen, & Liu, 2008, p. 485).

Problem-based learning emerged from the medical field in the 1950s as a response to criticism that traditional methods failed to prepare medical students for problem-solving in clinical settings. Since then, PBL has been implemented in K–12 settings (Barrows, 2000; Dochy et al., 2003; Hmelo-Silver, 2004). For example, Barrows and Kelson (1993) developed PBL curricula and teacher training programs for high school core subjects (see http://www.imsa.edu). Although the PBL research has received inconclusive results in the literature, some studies have shown promising results as effectiveness of PBL has been demonstrated in different content areas such as math (Kolodner et al., 2003), literature (Jacobsen & Spiro, 1994), history (Wieseman & Cadwell, 2005), macroeconomics (Mergendoller, Maxwell, & Bellismo, 2000), and microeconomics (Maxwell, Mergendoller, & Bellismo, 2005). In addition, PBL has been effective in urban, suburban, and rural schools (Delisle, 1997) as well as with a variety of student populations such as gifted (Gallagher, 1997) and low-income students (Stepien & Gallagher, 1993) and for students with below average verbal ability (Mergendoller et al., 2000).

Barrows and Kelson (1993) argued that the goals of PBL are to help students to (a) construct extensive and flexible knowledge base; (b) develop problem-solving skills; (c) develop self-directed, lifelong learning skills; (d) collaborate effectively; and (e) be intrinsically motivated to learn. Duch, Groh, and Allen (2001) pointed out the characteristics of good PBL consist of a problem that (a) motivates students to seek deeper understanding of a topic, (b) require students to reason and defend a position, (c) connects to prior knowledge and incorporate content objectives, (d) complex enough to ensure that students must work together to solve it, and (e) open-ended and engaging to draw students into the problem. According to Nilson (2010) a well-designed PBL allows students to develop skills such as working collaboratively and independently, leadership, oral and written communication, critical thinking, self-directed learning, applying content to real world examples, and research. Given the emerging research regarding the effectiveness of PBL, it is important to discuss the implementation for young children with and without disabilities.

Since the research on the effectiveness of PBL is mixed, researchers argue that elimination of confounding variables is important when conducting research and designing programs. Therefore, the creation of quality problems and learning opportunities are important to maximize student achievement. As a result, the content, context, and connection and researching, reasoning, and reflecting (3C3R) model was created to provide teachers with a conceptual framework to develop reliable and effective PBL opportunities for all levels of learners. The 3C3R model, developed by Hung (2006), was based his 9-step problem design process. According to Hung, the 3C3R models consists of core and process components. The core components are content, context, and connection, which are used to support content learning. Although some studies have demonstrated that students engaged in PBL performed lower than others on content knowledge measures, well-designed PBL problems require students to engage in content knowledge acquisition. Thus, teachers and PBL designers should use important content concepts from relevant standards to design PBL problems. Another consideration when developing PBL problems is the role and amount of content coverage (breadth vs depth) in the lesson design. Hung (2006) argued that problems should be designed to enrich student understanding of a subject area, and that poorly developed problems focus solely on problem-solving skills. Secondly, well designed PBL lessons require students to apply knowledge in clinical or real world contexts. In doing so, skills are often retained more easily and motivation is increased. Finally, to ensure that students generalize knowledge, problems should be connected to one another as opposed to independent of one another.

Process components consist of researching, reasoning, and reflecting and address learning and problem-solving skills. These components are similar to steps in problem-solving processes and/or scientific methods. Students begin with making sense of the problem and researching any necessary information. Reasoning requires students to apply content knowledge as well as develop problem-solving skills. Finally, in reflecting on the knowledge that they have gained, students can integrate and generalize knowledge and skills obtained to other areas. In addition to the 3C3R model, Hung (2009) described a 9-step process to help practitioners and PBL developers in designing optimal problems. The steps in the process are (a) set goals and objectives, (b) conduct content/task analysis, (c) analyze context specification, (d) select/generate PBL problem, (e) conduct correspondence analysis, (f) conduct calibration processes, (g) construct reflection component, and (h) examine inter-supporting relationships of

3C3R components. Although an in-depth discussion of each component is beyond the scope of this chapter, each is briefly described below.

The first step in Hung's (2009) 9-step process is determining the goals and objectives. Almost all instructions begin with selecting appropriate goals and objectives related to domain knowledge, problem solving, and self-directed learning skills. Once goals and objectives have been selected, Hung (2006) stated that developers should conduct content/task analysis. Content and task analyses are common to special education and examine all necessary steps in achieving a behavioral goal. When developing a problem for PBL, teachers should identify contents and procedures that the learner must possess. Once this has been completed, the teacher should analyze context specification, meaning that the context should be authentic. These authentic tasks should reflect context which learners would find appealing. Once the steps have been completed, the teacher can then begin selecting or generating a problem. The teacher should begin looking for real problems that learners might encounter in the given context. The fifth step is to construct a full description of the problem and analyze it. Hung (2009) explained that domain knowledge, problem-solving skills analysis, context analysis, and connection analysis are all aspects of problem affordance. The next step in the process is context correspondence analysis, which refers to adjusting the amount of contextual information in a problem. In order to maximize the effectiveness of PBL, teachers should avoid over and under contextualizing problems for learners.

The next step in the process is context component calibration. Context component calibration ensures that there is sufficient contextual information within the problem and influences the reasoning processes in which the student will be engaged. The seventh step in the process is researching and reasoning component calibration which is related to problem difficulty. Hung (2009) recommended creating missing links within the description of the problem, but when the missing links surpass the problem solving skills objectives, then the teacher should present this information to the students. The eighth step of the 9-step process is reflection. According to Hung (2009), reflection can be implemented by the PBL tutors and can be an ongoing process or can occur at the end of the problem. Reflections can occur through the use of journals, periodic progress meetings, or summative reflections. The last step in the 9–step process is to examine inter-supporting relationships of 3C3R components. As Hung (2009) pointed out, the components of the 3C3R Model are intended to be supportive of one another, and the interrelatedness of these components are necessary components of integrity and effectiveness of the model.

CONCLUSION

It is important for teachers to incorporate teaching methods that will help diverse students with and without disabilities access engaging and relevant curricula. Innovative teaching strategies allow educators to create current ideas and methods that will allow for the collaboration of technology and evidence-based strategies. However, being innovative may come with barriers. Such barriers may cause teachers not to buy-in and implement curricula that stifles the learning of students in and outside of the classroom. It is critical for teachers to work in an environment that promotes autonomy and effective teaching strategies for all learners. Innovative teaching methods that will help diverse learners are growth mindset and PBL. Growth mindset is when individuals believe hard work and training can lead to improved cognitive ability. This method includes an array of strategies that will shape the mindset of children during the learning process. Specifically, praise is a strategy that assists with the use of the learning strategy and the expected learning behaviors for certain tasks. PBL is an instructional method that focuses on students working collaboratively to solve open-ended, real world problems that have more than one solution. Research has shown that PBL is effective in different content areas as well as different demographics of school locations and student populations. To improve student achievement with PBL opportunities, Hung (2006) created the 3C3R model. This model provides teachers with a framework for creating PBL problems. Finally, it is imperative that teachers design instruction that is innovative and meet the needs of each learner regardless of the child's disability or capability. Teachers must consistently focus on ways to enhance the whole child and enhance their learning effectively.

REFERENCES

Aldhous, P. (2008). Free your mind and watch it grow. *New Scientist, 199*(2670), 44–45.

Barrows, H. S. (2000). *Problem-based learning applied to medical education.* Springfield: Southern Illinois University School of Medicine.

Barrows, H. S., & Kelson, A. (1993). *Problem-based learning in secondary education and the problem-based learning institute* (monograph). Springfield: Southern Illinois University School of Medicine.

Blackwell, L. S., Trzesniewski, K. H., & Dweck, C. S. (2007). Implicit theories of intelligence predict achievement across an adolescent transition: A longitudinal study and an intervention. *Child Development, 78*(1), 246–263.

Bradford, S., Shippen, M. E., Alberto, P. A., Houchins, D. E., & Flores, M. M. (2006). Using systematic instruction to teach decoding skills to middle school students with moderate intellectual disabilities. *Education and Training in Developmental Disabilities, 41*(4), 332–342.

Carlson, C., & Francis, D. (2002). Increasing the reading achievement of at-risk children through direct instruction: Evaluation of the Rodeo Institute for Teacher Excellence (RITE). *Journal of Education for Children Placed at Risk, 7*(2), 141–166.

Delisle, R. (1997). *How to use problem-based learning in the classroom.* Alexandria, VA: Association for Supervision and Curriculum Development.

Dochy, F., Segers, M., van den Bossche, P., & Gijbels, D. (2003). Effects of problem-based learning: A meta-analysis. *Learning and Instruction, 13*(5), 533–568.

Duch, B. J., Groh, S. E., & Allen, D. E. (Eds.). (2001). *The power of problem-based learning.* Sterling, VA: Stylus.

Dweck, C. (2006). *Mindset: The new psychology of success.* New York, NY: Random House.

Dweck, C. (2015). Carol Dweck revisits growth mindset. *Education Week 35*(5), 20–24.

Flores, M. M., Shippen, M. E., Alberto, P. A., & Crowe, L. (2004). Teaching letter-sound correspondence to students with moderate intellectual disabilities. *Journal of Direct Instruction, 4*(2), 173–188.

Fredrick, L. D., Keel, M. C., & Neel, J. H. (2002). Making the most of instructional time: Teaching reading at an accelerated rate to students at risk. *Journal of Direct Instruction, 2*(1), 57–62.

Gallagher, S. A. (1997). Problem-based learning: Where did it come from, what does it do, and where is it going? *Journal for the Education of the Gifted, 20*(4), 332–362.

Good, C., Aronson, J., & Inzlicht, M. (2003). Improving adolescents standardized test performance: An intervention to reduce the effects of stereotype threat. *Journal of Applied Developmental Psychology, 24*(6), 645–662.

Gunderson, E. A., Gripshover, S. J., Romero, C., & Dweck, C. S. (2013). Parent praise to 1- to 3-year-olds predicts children's motivational frameworks 5 years later. *Child Development 84*(5), 1526–1541.

Head, C., Flores, M., & Shippen, M. (2018). The effects of direct instruction on the reading comprehension skills of students with autism. *Education and Treatment of Autism and Developmental Disabilities, 53*(2), 176–191.

Hmelo-Silver, C. E. (2004). Problem-based learning: What and how do students learn? *Educational Psychology Review, 16*(3), 235–266.

Hung, W. (2006). The 3C3R model: A conceptual framework for designing problems in PBL. *Interdisciplinary Journal of Problem-Based Learning. 1*(1), 55–77.

Hung, W. (2009). The 9-step problem design process for problem-based learning: Application of the 3C3R model. *Educational Research Review, 4*(2), 118–141.

Hung, W., Jonassen, D. H., & Liu, R. (2008). Problem-based learning. In J. M. Spector, M. D. Merrill, J. van Merriënboer, & M. Driscoll (Eds.), *Handbook of research on educational communications and technology* (3rd ed., Vol. 1, pp. 485–506). New York, NY: Erlbaum.

Jacobsen, M., & Spiro, R. (1994). A framework for the contextual analysis of technology-based learning environments. *Journal of Computing in Higher Education, 5*(2), 2–32.

Kamins, M. L., & Dweck, C. S. (1999). Person versus process praise and criticism: Implications for contingent self-worth and coping. *Developmental Psychology 35*(3), 835–847.

Kolodner, J. L., Camp, P. J., Crismond, D., Fasse, B., Gray, J., Holbrook, J., . . . Ryan, M. (2003). Problem-based learning meets case-based reasoning in the middle-school science classroom: Putting learning by DesignTM into practice. *The Journal of the Learning Sciences, 12*(4), 495–547.

Lahey, J. (2015). *The gift of failure: How the best parents learn to let go so their children can succeed.* New York, NY: Harper Collins

Maxwell, N., Mergendoller, J. R., & Bellisimo, Y. (2005). Problem-based learning and high school macroeconomics: A comparative study of instructional methods. *The Journal of Economic Education, 36*(4), 315–331.

Mergendoller, J., Maxwell, N., & Bellisimo, Y. (2000). Comparing problem-based learning and traditional instruction in high school economics. *Journal of Educational Research, 93*(6), 374–382.

Morehead, J. (2015). Stanford University's Carol Dweck on the growth mindset and education. Retrieved from https://onedublin.org/2012/06/19/stanford-universitys-carol-dweck-on-the-growth-mindset-and-education/

Mueller, C. M., & Dweck, C. S. (1998). Praise for intelligence can undermine children's motivation and performance. *Journal of Personality and Social Psychology 75*(1), 33–52.

Nilson, L. B. (2010). *Teaching at its best: A research-based resource for college instructors* (2nd ed). San Francisco, CA: Jossey-Bass.

Shippen, M. E., Houchins, D. E., Steventon, C., & Sartor, D. L. (2005). A comparison of two direct instruction reading programs for urban middle school students. *Remedial and Special Education, 26*(3), 175–182.

Stepien, W. J., & Gallagher, S. A. (1993). Problem-based learning: As authentic as it gets. *Educational Leadership, 50*(7), 25–29.

Swanson, H. (1999). Instructional components that predict treatment outcomes for students with learning disabilities: Support for a combined strategy and direct instruction model. *Learning Disabilities Research, 14*(3), 129–140.

Torgesen, J., Alexander, A., Wagner, R., Rashotte, C., Voeller, K., & Conway, T. (2001). Intensive remedial instruction for children with severe reading disabilities: Immediate and long-term outcomes from two instructional approaches. *Journal of Learning Disabilities, 34*(1), 33–58.

Wieseman, K. C., & Cadwell, D. (2005). Local history and problem-based learning. *Social Studies and the Young Learner, 18*(1), 11–14.

CHAPTER 5

WHAT SCHOOL LEADERS CAN DO TO PROVIDE QUALITY EDUCATION FOR YOUNG CHILDREN WITH AUTISM

Alana Telesford, Floyd D. Beachum, and Carlos R. McCray

Autism spectrum disorder (ASD) is a neurodevelopmental disorder characterized by difficulties with social communication and interaction, and restricted and/or repetitive interests or behaviors (American Psychiatric Association, 2013). These difficulties persist through the life span and cause impairment across domains (e.g., academic, communication, social, and behavioral). The Diagnostic and Statistical Manual of Mental Disorders, 5th edition (DSM-V; APA, 2013) describes autism on a spectrum to capture the wide range of symptoms displayed by children who meet diagnostic criteria; the DSM-5 collapses autism, Asperger syndrome, and pervasive developmental disorder under the classification of ASD (Hart & More, 2013). The Centers for Disease Control and Prevention (2014) estimated that 1 in 68 children meet diagnostic criteria for ASD. More than 400,000 students with

Educating Young Children With and Without Exceptionalities, pages 61–77
Copyright © 2019 by Information Age Publishing

ASD enrolled in schools in the United States, all of whom exhibit a wide range of social, academic, and behavioral needs (Brock, Huber, Carter, Juarez, & Warren, 2014). Many of these students are being educated alongside their general education peers because of legislation (e.g., No Child Left Behind, 2001; Individuals With Disabilities in Education Act, 2004) advocating for education in the least restrictive environment (LRE; Sansosti & Sansosti, 2013). As such, all school professionals are urged to work with students with ASD and will be challenged to meet the diverse needs of this population (Brock et al., 2014; Stichter, Riley-Tillman, & Jimerson, 2016).

School leaders must understand hallmark characteristics of ASD, challenges that these students face in classrooms, challenges faced by educators of students with ASD, and challenges faced by families of children with ASD (Horrocks, White, & Roberts, 2008). School leaders can overcome these challenges and provide quality education to children with ASD by (a) promoting a culture of inclusion within their schools (Theoharis & Causton, 2014), (b) by providing professional development opportunities related to ASD to their staff (National Research Council, 2001), (c) holding staff accountable to using evidence-based practices (EBPs) that are individualized for students (Skokut, Robinson, Openden, & Jimerson, 2008), and (d) building strong partnerships between school staff and families of children with ASD (National Research Council, 2001). In addition, school leaders should be knowledgeable about how issues of culture impact service provision for students with ASD (Hart & More, 2013). This chapter focuses on effective ways in which school leaders can provide quality education to students with ASD.

INCLUSION

The rise in mainstreaming students with special education needs in general education classrooms, paired with increased legislation requiring accountability for student achievement, means that school leaders must be primarily concerned with creating inclusive school cultures (Theoharis & Causton, 2014). In inclusive schools, students with disabilities are equal to their general education peers and, as such, they have access to the general education curriculum, high quality instruction, and prosocial interactions with general education peers (Kantavong & Siyabaedya, 2010; Theoharis & Causton, 2014). Creating an inclusive culture within a school requires administrators to promote the presence (i.e., placing students with special education in general education classrooms), participation (i.e., individualized instruction), acceptance (i.e., inclusive attitudes and respect), and achievement (i.e., individualized goals and progress monitoring) of all students (Symes & Humphrey, 2011).

Educating students with ASD in segregated environments can be "developmentally toxic" (Strain, 2001, p. 31). Difficulty with social interactions is a hallmark characteristic of ASD and socialization is a key component of successful inclusion (Horrocks et al., 2008). By fully including students with ASD in general education settings, school leaders provide opportunities for these students to learn appropriate social and adaptive behavior skills, to develop meaningful reciprocated friendships with typically developing peers, and can lead to optimal post-school adjustment (Kim, Koegel, & Koegel, 2017; McCurdy & Cole, 2014). To ensure that students with ASD can access the curriculum and achieve in school, educators must have appropriately high expectations for them. Setting high expectations for students also builds trust between families and schools (Francis, Hill, Blue-Banning, Turnbull, & Haines, 2016). Students tend to fulfill teacher expectations of academic performance (i.e., if a teacher believes a student will not perform as well as their classmates, that student will likely fulfill this expectation). Although students with ASD exhibit some challenges in the regular education classroom, it is preferable that teachers maintain high expectations for these students rather than settle for academic and behavioral underachievement (Wilder, Dyches, Obiakor, & Algozzine, 2004).

School leaders should utilize paraprofessionals carefully. There is evidence to suggest that students with ASD who receive support from a one-to-one aide tend to underperform academically, receive less attention from their lead teacher, and become socially isolated from their peers (Symes & Humphrey, 2011). Paraprofessionals can be used to help manage classroom behavior for students with ASD so long as administrators and lead teachers ensure that these students remain academically and socially engaged (i.e., receive the same amount of teacher attention as general education peers and are not socially isolated). In addition, the IEP team should make sure that the student does not become over-reliant on the adult aide. It is important to have a plan in place for the student to eventually develop independence. For those students with ASD whose needs are better met in a self-contained special education classroom, administrators should ensure that these classrooms are not geographically isolated within a building from the general education population (i.e., all housed in the basement floor or within one wing of the building; Greene, 2015). Additionally, to foster a culture of inclusivity in schools, school leaders must shape the attitude of the entire school community; inclusive practices will not be successful if they are only embraced at the administrative level. All staff must have a shared understanding of the aims and logistics of inclusion which must be supported by actions, attitudes, and policies implemented by administrators (Capper & Frattura, 2009; Horrocks et al., 2008). Principals must clearly define and articulate a vision of an accepting and socially just school culture and continuously work to invest stakeholders (e.g., school staff and families) in this mission (Capper, Rodriguez, & McKinney, 2010). Principals and school staff must also convey this mission to students (Bloom, 2012) because if general education students are not equipped to understand, accept, and show compassion toward their special education peers, any staff-led initiatives toward inclusion will fail (Horrocks et al., 2008). This vision of inclusion should include: (a) school structure (i.e., the arrangement of teaching staff and students), (b) meeting the needs of all students within the general education curriculum (e.g., providing differentiated, evidence-based instruction in all classrooms), and (c) school climate (i.e., implementing procedures that allow for ongoing respectful dialogue between staff and students regarding inclusion; Theoharis & Causton, 2014).

After the vision has been defined, school leaders and their inclusion team should create a service delivery map to visually represent how services within the school are provided to students with ASD for the purpose of assessing the distribution of human resources. School teams can create a visual representation of general and special education classrooms, and related services. The service delivery map should include (a) staff members who are pulling students out of classrooms to provide services, (b) students who are educated in self-contained spaces, and (c) the distribution of paraprofessionals throughout the building to produce a complete picture of service provision. After the map has been created, school leaders should consider any structural changes that need to be made to create a more inclusive school. At the core of this analysis is the composition of classrooms. School leaders should arrange classrooms that are representative of the proportion of students with special education needs in the entire school. For example, if 10% of the students in a school have special education needs, then 10% of students in inclusive general education classrooms should be students with special education needs so as not to overload educators and to avoid clustering these students into one class. This will ensure that classrooms are a heterogeneous mix of learning abilities and of behavioral strengths and needs (Theoharis & Causton, 2014).

Creating an inclusive school requires mutual respect and collaboration amongst all members of the school community (e.g., educators, staff, students, and parents; Symes & Humphrey, 2011). As such, school leaders must fortify this sense of community amongst their staff as a prerequisite to promoting inclusion for students with ASD. When making educational decisions about the placement of, and interventions for, students with ASD, principals should consult with special educators, general educators, speech/language pathologists, occupational and physical therapists, behavior therapists, specialists, school psychologists, and parents (Greene, 2015). This ensures that educational decisions are not made in a top–down fashion. Rather, decision-making and intervention planning should be a collaborative process in which the opinions and expertise of all team members are valued. When members of the team disagree, alternative methods should be discussed as a group to ensure the best possible outcomes for students, educators, and families (Pierce & Tincani, 2007). In the end, an ongoing process of developing a culture of inclusion within a school is monitoring and adjusting as needed. Principals should elicit feedback on inclusion practices from staff, students, and families without abandoning the plan at the first signs of resistance. The inclusion team should work together to problem solve areas that are challenging or that are not producing optimal student outcomes, and should also celebrate, and continue to implement, successful strategies.

PROFESSIONAL DEVELOPMENT

Parents of children with ASD report greater satisfaction with their child's educational experience when they feel that teachers can manage their child's behavior and when teachers are knowledgeable and understanding of ASD (Starr & Foy, 2012). However, many educators do not receive formal training in ASD or in evidence-based strategies that promote academic, behavioral, and social success in this population (Theoharis, 2009). One notable barrier to additional training is limited class-release time for educators to develop their skill sets. Continuing education is often limited to didactic workshops that cover a broad range of topics, which may or may not include ASD, throughout the school year (Lerman, Vorndran, Addison, & Kuhn, 2004).

To have a direct impact on classroom practices, school leaders must allow teachers, paraprofessionals, administrators, and support staff to pursue professional development opportunities that specifically teach methods to support students with ASD. There is empirical evidence to suggest that brief, didactic instruction can help teachers acquire, maintain, and generalize the skills necessary to conduct stimulus preference assessments with students with ASD and to use incidental teaching skills (Lerman et al., 2004). This finding is reassuring because it suggests that teachers can, in limited time, learn and implement EBPs for students with ASD. Principals should ensure that all teaching staff (e.g., general educators, special educators, and specialists), support staff, lunch aides, and bus drivers receive ASD-specific training. Professional development opportunities should be targeted toward recognizing the diverse presentation of ASD symptoms (Hart & More, 2013) and using evidence-based strategies with students with ASD (e.g., co-teaching, differentiated instruction, addressing challenging behavior, and inquiry-based instruction; Theoharis & Causton, 2014). Trainings should also focus on critical programming elements, such as objective data collection, individualizing supports for each student, structuring classroom stimuli, and partnering with families (Maddox & Marvin, 2013). The intensity of professional development training can vary, with those staff members who work with students with ASD on a daily basis receiving yearlong support from their school leaders (Greene, 2015). Principals can utilize staff members with ASD expertise in their own building or district (e.g., school psychologists and behavior specialists) or use resources in the community, such as local universities or consultants from service agencies or local government offices, to provide training to staff. Skype calls and webinars are budget-friendly methods of utilizing outside resources (Greene, 2015).

Although didactic instruction has been demonstrated to be sufficient in impacting teacher practice, the most optimal student outcomes occur when there is performance-based assessment of teacher skills to ensure the students have mastered interventions and ongoing performance feedback to enhance the maintenance and generalization of target skills (Lerman et al., 2004). Thus, in addition to actively recruiting and hiring a high quality, diverse teaching staff, school leaders must also provide ongoing support to teaching staff so that they continue to develop their instructional practices (Capper et al., 2010). Obtaining feedback from a trained consultant or a mentor is also recommended (Maddox & Marvin, 2013). School leaders should also create opportunities for their staff to network with other education professionals. The National Staff Development Council was instituted to advocate for numerous, continuous opportunities for practitioners to network with each other so that they may learn and apply new strategies in their classrooms (Maddox & Marvin, 2013). In addition, school leaders and their staff must stay informed about current trends and best practices in special education. To accomplish this, they should all join local, state, and/or national professional organizations, read articles in peer-reviewed journals, and attend conferences, if possible. Educators can also sign up for free online subscriptions to emails and discussion threads related to serving students with ASD to stay up-to-date without spending instructional time attending conferences or professional development sessions (Hart & More, 2013). School leaders may also refer their staff to the Centers for Disease Control (http://www.cdc.gov/ncbddd/autism/educator.html) for resources specific for educators, including videos about the indicators of autism and suggestions for classroom planning.

FAMILY–SCHOOL PARTNERSHIPS

Partnerships between families and schools help increase academic, social, and behavioral outcomes for students with ASD (Blair, Lee, Cho, & Dunlap, 2011; Garbacz & McIntyre, 2016). In addition, parents of children with ASD report greater levels of satisfaction with their children's educational experience when there are high levels of collaboration and communication between the school and the family (Starr & Foy, 2012). Families are more likely to support school-based strategies, and to implement home recommendations, when they believe that their family structure and belief system are being respected (Skokut et al., 2008). School administrators, specifically, principals, have been identified by parents of children with and without disabilities to be essential in creating a culture of trust and community between the school and the families they serve (Francis et al., 2016). Building trust between families and school staff is critical for problem solving throughout the child's life. After consulting with 11 focus groups of parents of children with and without disabilities, Francis, Hill, Blue-Banning, Turnbull, and Haines (2016) identified five factors that contribute to trusting partnerships, namely: (a) school culture of inclusion; (b) positive administrative leadership; (c) attributes of positive partnerships; (d) opportunities for family involvement; and (e) positive outcomes for all students, including those with disabilities. Parents reported that "school principals who were friendly, involved, and focused on positive student outcomes influenced school culture and established trust and involvement among families" (Francis et al., 2016, p. 290). To promote trust between the school and families, principals can display benevolence, honesty, openness, reliability, and competence (Tschannen-Moran, 2014).

Frequent communication with families is essential to building partnerships necessary to serve students with ASD. It is preferable that communication is not only when the child is having academic or behavioral challenges in school, but that it is also utilized to celebrate student success. School leaders should offer families a variety of modes of communication (e.g., phone calls, emails, Skype, and home visits) as well as flexibility when these communications occur. This conveys to the family that the school is interested in familial preferences and that families are valued partners in their child's education (Hart & More, 2013). Regular communication helps to build trust, and focusing on the strengths, as well as the needs, of the child will promote positive collaboration (Starr & Foy, 2012). Sharing information about autism and available services during these communications can also build family-school connections (Hart & Moore, 2013). School leaders can (a) provide families with information about community services for children with ASD, (b) send progress updates home about their child, and (c) share successful classroom management techniques. Multidisciplinary team meetings and individualized education program (IEP) meetings are formal opportunities to collaborate with families to determine appropriate goals for their child. Educators and specialists (e.g., special education teachers, speech/language therapists, and occupational therapists) should prepare progress monitoring data in formats that are easy for families to understand. Principals can encourage educators to communicate with families informally to review data on classroom behavior and academics. School leaders and school staff may also conduct needs assessments with families of students with ASD to assess family knowledge of ASD and to determine if there are any resources that the family can utilize to meet these needs (Hart & More, 2013). This assessment can be achieved by performing home visits with the family to gain a comprehensive perspective on the child's functional levels (Greene, 2015). Additionally, school leaders should encourage families to monitor younger siblings of children with ASD for symptomatology because prevalence of ASD amongst siblings is approximately 20% (Hart & More, 2013).

EVIDENCE-BASED PRACTICES

School leaders can impact educational outcomes for students with ASD by ensuring that their staff members are implementing EBP (Skokut et al., 2008). The use of EBP in schools has been required by recent legislature (i.e., IDEA, NCLB; Skokut et al., 2008; Williams, Johnson, & Sukhodolsky, 2005). As such, schools should only be considering interventions that have empirical support. Some scholars disagree about what constitutes "evidence," but, it is generally agreed that interventions supported by strong qualitative studies, single subject designs, and group designs can be used with students with ASD (Skokut et al., 2008). All strategies employed in schools with students should have experimental, rather than anecdotal support. It is also preferred that strategies have demonstrated effects in real classrooms under typical conditions (Pierce & Tincani, 2007). School administrators tend to focus on the implementation of EBPs to address problem behaviors in students with ASD; this may be due to school leaders' role as a manager of crises. Empirically supported instructional practices that target functional or academic skills are critically needed to serve these students (Brock et al., 2014).

Applied behavior analysis (ABA) is one of the most empirically supported, and most widely used, methods of intervening with students with ASD (Reichow, 2012). It is a strategy in which educators systematically manipulate the classroom environment to increase the likelihood that a desired target behavior will be emitted by a student or students (Cooper, 1982). Many educators and school leaders have general knowledge of basic behavioral principles (Cooper, 1982); but oftentimes, these professionals do not receive formal training in ABA during their studies (Loiacono & Valenti, 2010). Those professionals who are trained in ABA and in positive behavior support (PBS) can ensure that students with ASD enjoy the most optimal outcomes. According to the manual created by the National Autism Center (NAC) in 2015, the 14 interventions for students with ASD with the most empirical support are (a) behavioral interventions, (b) cognitive behavioral intervention packages, (c) comprehensive behavioral treatment for young children, (d) language training, (e) modeling, (f) natural teaching strategies, (g) parent training packages, (h) peer training packages, (i) pivotal response training, (j) schedules, (k) social scripts, (l) self-management, (m) social skills packages, and (n) story-based interventions. This manual is available for free electronic download (see http://www.nationalautismcenter.org/resources/). School leaders should refer to the NAC for more detailed descriptions and procedures, and for additional resources for educators, parents, and practitioners that provide guidance on addressing the diverse needs of students with ASD. School leaders are reminded that in addition to using these aforementioned strategies, it is also necessary to measure the fidelity of intervention implementation, the acquisition of target skills in teachers, and student outcomes. It is important that educators do not simply select elements from evidence-based interventions to create a comprehensive intervention plan. This practice creates a "buffet of choices" and each element may not work together in the way that has been supported by the literature. There is some evidence to suggest that taking an eclectic approach may result in less favorable outcomes for students with ASD; as such, educators and school leaders should exercise this practice with caution (Skokut et al., 2008). Multiple intervention elements can be used if instructors are using a behavior analytic strategy to determine which elements are prompting meaningful change in student behavior (Stichter et al., 2016).

When implementing and evaluating an intervention, staff should develop an action plan which includes explicit strategies for evaluating and modifying the intervention to achieve optimal outcomes. The action plan should also include explicit data collection procedures (e.g., what data will be collected, who will collect the data, how will the data be collected, and for how long the data will be collected; Pierce & Tincani, 2007). School leaders are responsible for ensuring that educators implement EBPs with fidelity. Principals must "make it clear that when a support has been shown to help a student, it should be implemented in every class period throughout the child's day, not just at an individual teacher's discretion" (Greene, 2015, p. 38). Empirically supported interventions will not be successful in the classroom if they are implemented without fidelity. As such, school leaders must ensure that educators and staff are adequately trained in the methods they are using and that implementation data is being collected and analyzed (Skokut et al., 2008). Clearly, Dr. Stephen Shore's assertion that "if you've met one person with autism, you've met one person with autism" (Shields, 2015) is key to designing intervention plans. Within a student's IEP, educators should employ flexibility so that goals and instruction reflect the changing needs of the student at each level in their life (Greene, 2015;

Symes & Humphrey, 2011). School leaders should use data when making decisions about a child's educational placement, or about the effectiveness of interventions (Greene, 2015). There is no one intervention that will work for every student with ASD. In addition to individual student factors, teachers should also consider the local context and available resources when selecting or modifying interventions for students with ASD (Skokut et al., 2011). Educators must be aware of the interplay of variables that can affect the efficacy of an intervention at the universal level (e.g., those that are common to every child), at the group level (e.g., those that are common to pupils with ASD), and at the individual level (e.g., those that are typical for the student at hand; Symes & Humphrey, 2011).

CULTURAL CONSIDERATIONS

School leaders must also consider issues of culture as it relates to serving students with ASD. Recently, researchers have found racial/ethnic disparities in the diagnosis and treatment of ASD. Non-Hispanic White children are more likely to receive a diagnosis of ASD than Black or Hispanic children and children with ASD from racial/ethnic minority backgrounds receive less specialized services than their White counterparts (Emerson, Morrell, & Neece, 2016). These disparities will impact service delivery for diverse students with ASD in school settings. For example, White children are 30% more likely to receive an ASD diagnosis than non-Hispanic Black children (Emerson et al., 2016). In addition, children from ethnic minority groups are less likely to receive a diagnosis of ASD at an early age in the United States (Mandell, Listerud, Levy, & Pinto-Martin, 2002; Mandell, Novak, & Zubritsky, 2005; Mandell et al., 2009). Emerson, Morrell, and Neece (2016) analyzed data from the 2011–2012 National Survey of Children's Health and found that the age of ASD diagnosis was predicted by race, symptom severity, and having a consistent source of medical care. Black and Hispanic children who had a consistent source of care were still at risk for a delayed diagnosis of ASD. Black children were 2.6 times less likely to be diagnosed with ASD on their first visit to a healthcare provider (HCP), and they are also referred to specialty care later than White children. After being referred to a specialist, Black children required more visits to these specialty care providers than White children before receiving a diagnosis. Mandell et al. (2002) studied a sample of Medicaid-eligible children and adolescents in Philadelphia county and used linear regression to examine the relationship between race, age at diagnosis of ASD, time spent in mental health treatment, and the number of physician visits until a diagnosis was determined. They found that (a) White children were diagnosed at a younger age than Black children, (b) that White children entered mental health treatment earlier than Black children, and (c) that Black children required a greater number of physician visits before receiving a diagnosis. Of children who met criteria for ASD, only 25% of White children also met criteria for an intellectual disability (ID) while 48% of Black children and 38% of Hispanic children met criteria for ID (Emerson et al., 2016). There is also evidence which indicates Hispanic children are diagnosed a full year later than White children (Magaña, Lopez, Aguinaga, & Morton, 2013). To a large measure, the way in which children receive a diagnosis of ASD also varies by race. Children from racial/ethnic minority backgrounds tend to rely on the special education process in their child's school for autism identification (Travers, Tincani, & Krezmien, 2013). Emerson and colleagues (2016) conducted a multiple linear regression using data from the 2011 National Survey of Children's Health to examine the effects of race, symptom severity, and access to a consistent source of healthcare on the age of diagnosis of ASD. They found that only one in five White children are diagnosed with ASD by a primary care HCP, indicating that most White children receive an ASD label from a diagnostic specialist such as a psychiatrist or developmental pediatrician. In contrast, over one third of Black children receive a diagnosis of ASD from a primary care provider. Emerson and colleagues (2016) cautiously conclude that the delay in diagnosing Black children with ASD can be attributed to slower and/or less frequent referrals by a regular physician to healthcare specialists. The source of this disparity is multifaceted. In the end, observed ethnic differences in autism diagnosis are due to both provider and parent behaviors (Emerson et al., 2016).

Mandell and colleagues (2002) postulated that lack of a consistent source of healthcare, culturally different expectations for seeking and utilizing mental health or behavioral treatment, and differences in symptom presentation may all contribute to the under-diagnosis of culturally and linguistically diverse (CLD) children with ASD. It is possible that HCPs are not referring Black or Hispanic children to specialists at the same rate at which they refer White children. It is also possible that parental initiation for a diagnosis or follow-through on specialized services is different in White versus CLD populations. Black and Hispanic parents tend to follow up on referrals slower than White parents (Zuckerman et al., 2011), and it has also been found that these families face more socioeconomic, scheduling, and transportation barriers to attend specialist appointments than White families (Broder-Fingert et al., 2013; Kalb et al., 2012). Another possible reason for observed disparities in ASD diagnosis is the heterogeneous presentation of ASD across racial/ethnic groups. Sell, Giarelli, Blum, Hanlon, and Levy (2012) found that Black children were more likely to present with object fixation and adherence to inflexible routines and that White children were more likely to present with abnormal motor development and unusual response to sensory input. In addition, Becerra and colleagues (2014) found that children from CLD backgrounds who met criteria for ASD were more likely to present with extreme emotional responses and expressive language deficits than White children who met criteria. It is possible that HCPs are trained to attribute these emotional responses and language delays to other conditions (Emerson et al., 2016). Family factors also contribute to this disparity. Different cultures may perceive ASD symptoms differently and these views can delay initial evaluation and affect help-seeking behaviors and service use. Put another way, families from different cultural backgrounds may observe symptoms of ASD through a cultural lens. For example, a child who is a late talker may not be a concern in families who value children watching and listening to adults or silence/think time during conversations with adults (Hart & More, 2013). It is also possible that families from different cultural backgrounds may not have the vocabulary to define, and therefore understand, ASD and the implications it has for their child's behavior and development (Wilder et al., 2004).

Help-seeking behaviors of CLD families differ from those utilized by the majority culture (Mandell et al., 2002). Thomas, Ellis, McLaurin, Daniels, and Morrissey (2007) found that CLD parents, parents with lower levels of education, and families living in non-metropolitan areas have limited access to care. Magaña and colleagues (2013) found that Latino children received fewer specialty healthcare services, and had higher unmet service needs than White children; this difference has been found to persist even when controlling for severity of symptoms (Magaña, Parish, & Son, 2015). Even when services are available, the degree to which they are utilized vary by culture. For instance, Black families rely heavily on the social support of families, friends, and religious groups, and may utilize these resources before seeking out professional assistance (Hart & More, 2013). To address systemic differences in diagnosis and treatment seeking, school leaders and educators must first be knowledgeable about cultural composition of their student body, and require their educators to do the same. Hart and More (2013) noted that educators can accomplish this by participating in community cultural activities and by attending diversity trainings or workshops offered in the community. They also recommended the Educational Alliance at Brown University (see http://www.alliance.brown.edu/tdl/index.shtml) as a resource for educators to increase their cultural understanding. School personnel can invite family members or community members from various cultural groups to educate students and staff about how members of that group tend to perceive education, ASD, and mental and behavioral health treatment (Hart & More, 2013).

Educational leaders should remain aware of the heterogeneous presentation of ASD symptoms and should examine presenting symptoms in students through a cultural lens. This is easier when educators and administrators are familiar with common beliefs of the diverse families they serve (McCray & Beachum, 2014). For example, a student who avoids eye contact with and responds to yes/no questions with gestures rather than words may be displaying signs of ASD or they may be behaving in the way that is expected of them in their home (Wilder et al., 2004). For more intensive language needs, school leaders should provide bilingual or English language learning support so that the child can have access to the curriculum in both languages (Wilder et al., 2004). Additionally, school leaders can provide materials related to ASD warning signs, treatment options, and advocacy strategies in the language that families are most fluent in and also provide classroom instruction in the language that is most accessible to the student. When students with ASD come from households in which the primary language is not English, school leaders should ensure that students are comprehensively assessed for language and communication needs in the language that is most appropriate for them. These assessments should utilize norm-referenced instruments and assessment should be ongoing throughout the child's educational career (Wilder et al., 2004). Depending on the language needs of the child, school leaders should empower educators to use strategies such as picture communication systems, sign language, or other types of alternative communication systems.

CONCLUSION

Within their schools, the attitudes and behaviors of principals serve as models for school staff and for students. Principals embody a vision of socially just education through explicit means (e.g., implementation decisions, resource allocation, and supervision of personnel) as well as implicitly through their actions or symbolic gestures (Horrocks et al., 2008). School leaders play critical roles in providing quality education to students with ASD. By creating a culture of inclusion, holding their entire staff accountable to implementing individualized, EBPs with fidelity, creating collaborative family–school partnerships, and remaining culturally conscious of students' diverse range of needs, school leaders can ensure that students with ASD will have optimal outcomes. Clearly, school leaders who use culturally relevant perspectives increase relevance, rigor, and respect for students (Beachum & McCray, 2011). Culturally proficient school leaders realize the impact of education in the lives of youth and, as such, understand how their roles impact student trajectories (Ladson-Bilings, 1995; McCray & Beachum, 2014; Milner, 2010). This mindset helps to motivate school leaders and related professionals to stay current with empirically supported methods of serving students with special needs. In addition, this mindset allows for purposeful collaboration with parents and guardians, advocates, and private practice professionals or service providers.

REFERENCES

American Psychiatric Association. (2013). *Diagnostic and statistical manual of mental disorders: DSM-5*. Washington, DC: American Psychiatric Association.

Beachum, F. D., & McCray, C. R. (2011). *Cultural collision and collusion: Reflections on hip-hop culture, values, and schools*. New York, NY: Peter Lang.

Becerra, T. A., Von Ehrenstein, O. S., Heck, J. E., Olsen, J., Arah, O. A., Jeste, S. S., . . . & Ritz, B. (2014). Autism spectrum disorders and race, ethnicity, and nativity: A population-based study. *Pediatrics, 134*(1), 63–71. doi: 10.1542/peds.2013-3928.

Blair, K. S. C., Lee, I. S., Cho, S. J., & Dunlap, G. (2011). Positive behavior support through family–School collaboration for young children with autism. *Topics in Early Childhood Special Education, 31*(1), 22–36. doi: 10.1177/0271121410377510

Bloom, M. I. (2012). What parents want principals to know about autism. *Principal, 91*(3), 20–23.

Brock, M. E., Huber, H. B., Carter, E. W., Juarez, A. P., & Warren, Z. E. (2014). Statewide assessment of professional development needs related to educating students with autism spectrum disorder. *Focus on Autism and Other Developmental Disabilities, 29*(2), 67–79. doi: 10.1177/1088357614522290

Broder-Fingert, S., Shui, A., Pulcini, C. D., Kurowski, D., & Perrin, J. M. (2013). Racial and ethnic differences in subspecialty service use by children with autism. *Pediatrics, 132*, 94–100. doi:10.1542/peds.2012-3886

Capper, C. A., & Frattura, E. M. (2009). *Meeting the needs of students of all abilities* (2nd ed). Thousand Oaks, CA: Corwin.

Capper, C. A., Rodriguez, M. A., & McKinney, S. A. (2010). Leading beyond disability: Integrated, socially just schools and districts. In C. Marshall & M. Oliva (Eds.), *Leadership for social justice: Making revolutions in education* (2nd ed., pp. 175–193). Boston, MA: Pearson.

Centers for Disease Control. (2014). Prevalence of autism spectrum disorders among children aged 8 years: Autism and developmental disabilities monitoring network, 11 sites, United States, 2010. *MMWR Surveillance Summaries 63*(2), 1–22.

Cooper, J. O. (1982). Applied behavior analysis in education. *Theory Into Practice, 21*(2), 114–118. doi: 10.1080/00405848209542992

Emerson, N. D., Morrell, H. E., & Neece, C. (2016). Predictors of age of diagnosis for children with autism spectrum disorder: The role of a consistent source of medical care, race, and condition severity. *Journal of Autism and Developmental Disorders, 46*(1), 127–138. doi:10.1007/s10803-015-2555-x

Francis, G. L., Hill, C., Blue-Banning, M., Turnbull, A. P., & Haines, S. J. (2016). Culture in inclusive schools: Parental perspectives on trusting family-professional partnerships. *Education and Training in Autism and Developmental Disabilities, 51*(3), 281–293.

Garbacz, S. A., & McIntyre, L. L. (2016). Conjoint behavioral consultation for children with Autism Spectrum Disorder. *School Psychology Quarterly, 31*(4), 450–466. doi:10.1037/spq0000114

Greene, K. (2015). A school leader's guide to autism. *Scholastic Administrator, 15*(1), 36–41.

Hart, J. E., & More, C. (2013). Strategies for addressing the disproportionate representation of diverse students with autism spectrum disorder. *Intervention in School and Clinic, 48*(3), 167–173. doi:10.1177/1053451212454168

Horrocks, J. L., White, G., & Roberts, L. (2008). Principals' attitudes regarding inclusion of children with autism in Pennsylvania public schools. *Journal of Autism and Developmental Disorders, 38*(8), 1462–1473. doi:10.1007/s10803-007-0522-x

Kalb, L. G., Freedman, B., Foster, C., Menon, D., Landa, R., Kishfy, L., & Law, P. (2012). Determinants of appointment absenteeism at an outpatient pediatric autism clinic. *Journal of Developmental & Behavioral Pediatrics, 33*(9), 685–697. doi:10.1097/DBP.0b013e31826c66ef

Kantavong, P., & Sivabaedya, S. (2010). A professional learning program for enhancing the competency of students with special needs. *International Journal of Whole Schooling, 6*(1), 53–62.

Kim, S., Koegel, B., & Kern Koegel, L. (2017). Social inclusion for students with Autism Spectrum Disorder. In *Supporting social inclusion for students with Autism Spectrum Disorders: Insights from research and practice* (pp. 21–32). New York, NY: Routledge.

Ladson-Billings, G. (1995). But that's just good teaching! The case for culturally relevant pedagogy. *Theory Into Practice, 34*(3), 159–165.

Lerman, D. C., Vorndran, C. M., Addison, L., & Kuhn, S. C. (2004). Preparing teachers in evidence-based practices for young children with autism. *School Psychology Review, 33*(4), 510–526.

Loiacono, V., & Valenti, V. (2010). General education teachers need to be prepared to co-teach the increasing number of children with autism in inclusive settings. *International Journal of Special Education, 25*(3), 24–32.

Maddox, L. L., & Marvin, C. A. (2013). A preliminary evaluation of a statewide professional development program on autism spectrum disorders. *Teacher Education and Special Education, 36*(1), 37–50. doi:10.1177/0888406412463827

Magaña, S., Lopez, K., Aguinaga, A., & Morton, H. (2013). Access to diagnosis and treatment services among Latino children with autism spectrum disorders. *Intellectual and Developmental Disabilities, 51*(3), 141–153. doi:10.1352/1934-9556-51.3.141

Magaña, S., Parish, S. L., & Son, E. (2015). Have racial and ethnic disparities in the quality of health care relationships changed for children with developmental disabilities and ASD? *American Journal on Intellectual and Developmental Disabilities, 120*(6), 504–513. doi:10.1352/1944-7558-120.6.504

Mandell, D. S., Listerud, J., Levy, S. E., & Pinto-Martin, J. A. (2002). Race differences in the age at diagnosis among Medicaid-eligible children with autism. *Journal of the American Academy of Child & Adolescent Psychiatry, 41*(12), 1447–1453. doi:10.1097/00004583-200212000-00016

Mandell, D. S., Novak, M. M., & Zubritsky, C. D. (2005). Factors associated with age of diagnosis among children with autism spectrum disorders. *Pediatrics, 116*(6), 1480–1486.

Mandell, D. S., Wiggins, L. D., Carpenter, L. A., Daniels, J., DiGuiseppi, C., Durkin, M. S.,...& Shattuck, P. T. (2009). Racial/ethnic disparities in the identification of children with autism spectrum disorders. *American Journal of Public Health, 99*(3), 493–498. doi:10.2105/AJPH.2007.131243

McCray, C. R., & Beachum, F. D. (2014). *School leadership in a diverse society: Helping schools prepare all students for success.* Charlotte, NC: Information Age.

McCurdy, E. E., & Cole, C. L. (2014). Use of a peer support intervention for promoting academic engagement of students with autism in general education settings. *Journal of Autism and Developmental Disorders, 44*(4), 883–893. doi:10.1007/s10803-013-1941-5

Milner, H. R. (2010). *Start where you are but don't stay there: Understanding diversity, opportunity gaps, and teaching in today's classrooms.* Cambridge, MA: Harvard Education Press.

National Research Council. (2001). *Educating children with autism.* Washington, DC: National Academy Press. doi:10.17226/10017

Pierce, T., & Tincani, M. (2007). Beyond consumer advocacy: Autism spectrum disorders, effective instruction, and public schools. *Intervention in School and Clinic, 43*(1), 47–51.

Reichow, B. (2012). Overview of meta-analyses on early intensive behavioral intervention for young children with autism spectrum disorders. *Journal of Autism and Developmental Disorders, 42*(4), 512–520. doi:10.1007/s10803-011-1218-9

Sansosti, F. J., & Sansosti, J. M. (2013). Effective school-based service delivery for students with autism spectrum disorders: Where we are and where we need to go. *Psychology in the Schools, 50*(3), 229–244. doi:10.1002/pits.21669

Sell, N. K., Giarelli, E., Blum, N., Hanlon, A. L., & Levy, S. E. (2012). A comparison of autism spectrum disorder DSM-IV criteria and associated features among African American and white children in Philadelphia County. *Disability and Health Journal, 5*(1), 9–17. doi:10.1016/j.dhjo.2011.08.002

Shields, M. (2015). Transition to tertiary: Building bridges in secondary school, making it work for young people with Asperger's Syndrome. *Special Education Perspectives, 24*(1), 7–14.

Skokut, M., Robinson, S., Openden, D., & Jimerson, S. R. (2008). Promoting the social and cognitive competence of children with autism: Interventions at school. *California School Psychologist, 13*(1), 93–108.

Starr, E. M., & Foy, J. B. (2012). In parents' voices: The education of children with autism spectrum disorders. *Remedial and Special Education, 33*(4), 207–216. doi:10.1177/0741932510383161

Stichter, J. P., Riley-Tillman, T. C., & Jimerson, S. R. (2016). Assessing, understanding, and supporting students with autism at school: Contemporary science, practice, and policy. *School Psychology Quarterly, 31*(4), 443–449. doi:10.1037/spq0000184

Strain, P. S. (2001). Empirically based social skill intervention: A case for quality-of-life improvement. *Behavioral Disorders, 27*(1), 30–36.

Symes, W., & Humphrey, N. (2011). School factors that facilitate or hinder the ability of teaching assistants to effectively support pupils with autism spectrum disorders (ASDs) in mainstream secondary schools. *Journal of Research in Special Educational Needs, 11*(3), 153–161. doi:10.1111/j.1471-3802.2011.01196.x

Theoharis, G. (2009). *The school leaders our children deserve: Seven keys to equity, social justice, and school reform.* New York, NY: Teachers College Press.

Theoharis, G., & Causton, J. (2014). Leading inclusive reform for students with disabilities: A school-and systemwide approach. *Theory Into Practice, 53*(2), 82–97. doi:10.1080/00405841.2014.885808

Thomas, K. C., Ellis, A. R., McLaurin, C., Daniels, J., & Morrissey, J. P. (2007). Access to care for autism-related services. *Journal of Autism and Developmental Disorders, 37*(10), 1902–1912. doi:10.1007/s10803-006-0323-7

Travers, J. C., Tincani, M., & Krezmien, M. P. (2013). A multiyear national profile of racial disparity in autism identification. *The Journal of Special Education, 47*(1), 41–49. doi:10.1177/0022466911416247

Tschannen-Moran, M. (2014). *Trust matters: Leadership for successful schools* (2nd ed.). San Francisco, CA: Jossey-Bass.

Wilder, L. K., Dyches, T. T., Obiakor, F. E., & Algozzine, B. (2004). Multicultural perspectives on teaching students with autism. *Focus on Autism and Other Developmental Disabilities, 19*(2), 105–113. doi:10.1177/10883576040190020601

Williams, S. K., Johnson, C., & Sukhodolsky, D. G. (2005). The role of the school psychologist in the inclusive education of school-age children with autism spectrum disorders. *Journal of School Psychology, 43*(2), 117–136. doi:10.1016/j.jsp.2005.01.002

Zuckerman, K. E., Nelson, K., Bryant, T. K., Hobrecker, K., Perrin, J. M., & Donelan, K. (2011). Specialty referral communication and completion in the community health center setting. *Academic Pediatrics, 11*(4), 288–296. doi:10.1016/j.acap.2011.03.002

CHAPTER 6

EMPOWERING PARENTS OF YOUNG ATYPICAL LEARNERS

Mateba K. Harris

For many families, welcoming a new baby into the household can all together be a jubilant and challenging time. While all parents must adjust and adapt to the physical and emotional demands of parenting a young child, it is more likely that parents of young, atypical students may also experience denial, grief, stress, or anger (Koch, 2016). Having a child with a disability can be very stressful for parents. These parents go through stages when they initially find out their child is a student with a disability. According to Faerstein (1981), parents primarily experience reactions such as denial, overprotection, guilt, and blame, and possibly followed by masochistic or martyristic reactions, withdrawal, regression, and low self-esteem. Parenting a child with a disability means parents are charged with familiarizing themselves with the special education process, including referrals for services, signing consent to evaluate documentation, and becoming an active participant of the individualized education program (IEP) process (McCloskey, 2010). To assist parents of students with disabilities with some

Educating Young Children With and Without Exceptionalities, pages 79–90
Copyright © 2019 by Information Age Publishing
All rights of reproduction in any form reserved.

of the stressors and emotional outputs from having a child with a disability, Fareo (2015) suggested less emphasis be placed on the stressors of having a child with a disability, and instead provide resources and relationships for families to cope and build stability. Since schools and families share the responsibility of ensuring students obtain information and develop life-long skills to live successfully in society (Cardona, Sachin, & Canfiled-Davis, 2012), setting up interventions and resources for families beginning with early childhood programs will benefit all stakeholders.

EARLY CHILDHOOD PREPAREDNESS

Within the first few years of a child's life, neurological foundations for cognitive abilities are set (Children Now, 2014). However, the development of children is not only biological; children develop in response to social and cultural experiences (Adair, 2010). Adentwi (2005) stated that how we approach young children largely depends on what we believe children are like, and how they behave and act in life. Children's experiences in early childhood shape and influence the rest of their lives. In fact, early childhood education is one of the most determinative factors of an individual's life (Frabutt & Waldron, 2013). In addition to early childhood programs shaping children for the future, Ntumi (2016) added that preschool teachers represent key roles in early childhood curriculum implementation. These responsibilities may include respecting cultural diversity, child guidance and discipline, implementing appropriate curriculum and teacher and learning methods, developing reciprocal relationships and with families, and providing guidance and discipline. Early childhood programs will only meet their mission if they reach and service students at special risk of facing challenges in school (Adams & McDaniels, 2012). Unfortunately, many students do not receive the supports necessary for developing linguistic skills (Lehman, 2017) and cultural capital (Obiakor, Harris, Offor, & Beachum, 2010) needed to access teachers and curriculum. Furthermore, many culturally and linguistically diverse (CLD) families are not consulted on how schools might best meet the needs of their young learners (Cardona et al., 2012). The National Association for the Education of Young Children (NAEYC) and The office of Head Start (OHS) highlighted that early childhood programs construct environments and learning opportunities that respect diversity; support connections between their children, their families, and their communities, and safeguard children's cultural identities and home languages (NAEYC, 2009; OHS, 2008). Parents of atypical learners spend a great deal of time interacting and communication with teachers, and the relationships may be multifaceted and tenuous (Koch,

2016). Therefore, establishing positive relationships, and referring to families for suggestions are significant in meeting the needs of young learners. See case of Dylan below to know what happens when schools teachers and professionals fail to do the right thing.

CASE OF DYLAN

Dylan was a three year old attending an early childhood program. His mom, a single parent, living in the city, showed enthusiasm and support for her first son attending school. She attended parent events offered at the school, including parent teacher conferences, and often times served as a room mother, volunteering when her schedule allowed. Education was very important to Dylan's mother. She taught Dylan how to read at a very early age. In fact, by the age of three, upon entry to the early childhood program, Dylan was reading at a first grade reading level. His teachers, in the early childhood program initially raved about Dylan's ability to read and his willingness to read to the class. However, during the first semester, the teacher began to express concerns for Dylan's behavior. She told Dylan's mom that her son had trouble focusing during circle time, and he did not want to sit down and listen within the group, for an extended amount of time. Although Dylan's mom did not agree with the presumptions of his teacher, she trusted the professional and agreed to have him evaluated by his doctor for attention deficit disorder.

The above account is a common experience of parents of young, atypical learners. The school did not take the initiative to work with the parent for her expertise with Dylan. Instead, they made hasty recommendations for her to have Dylan evaluated for special education services.

PARENTAL ENGAGEMENT AND RESPONSIBILITY

Parental engagement, often used interchangeably with parent involvement comprises behaviors that directly or indirectly support children's experiences both at home and at school (Pomerantz, Moorman, & Litwack, 2007). However, parental responsibility is a central concept in all special education laws. This means that (a) parents must behave dutifully towards their children and (b) the responsibility for childcare belongs to parents, not the state (Eekelaar, 1994). Earlier, Christmon (1990) noted that parental responsibility is influenced by one's own role, expectations, and self images. Squelch (2006) argued that it is the responsibility of parents to nurture, discipline, and socialize their children. Additionally, Squelch (2006) argued that parents have a duty of care and are co-responsible, alongside with teachers for their children's education, and concluded that parents are responsible for their student's social, educational, and moral developments; and for ensuring "that their children comply with the school's code of conduct" (p. 249).

Researchers have noted that parental involvement positively influences student outcomes in school. Student achievement, higher grades, and favorable opinions are a few emphasized (Bempechat, 1992; Brandon, 2007; Comer & Haynes, 1991; Epps, 1995; Henderson & Mapp, 2002; Hill & Kraft, 2003; Obiakor, Harris, & Beachum, 2009). As indicated earlier, many parents face exclusion from the decision-making process, despite efforts of federal, local, and state mandates (Adair, 2010). Parents' accessibility to their children's progress and teachers' suggestions and recommendations increase parental engagement and student achievement. It is not uncommon to see parents get their students involved in Head Start programs or other early childhood programs to help their children prepare for entrance into 4- and 5-year-old kindergarten educational settings. These actions are in accord with what Clark (1983) classically termed as "parent involvement," and defined parent involvement as parent child interactions aimed at helping students with their homework, expressing expectations of school performance, and creating supportive learning environments within the home. Grolnick and Slowiaczek (1994) suggested three different types of parental involvement in the education of students, namely:

1. school involvement, which refers to parental participation in school activities such as attending school functions, and out of school activities such as helping students with their homework;
2. cognitive-intellectual involvement, which refers to engaging students in intellectually -stimulating activities like reading with the students; and
3. personal involvement, which refers to knowing what, is going on at the school.

In special education, parent involvement is one of the main components of the 1990 Individuals With Disabilities Education Act (IDEA; Harry, 2008). IDEA gives parents the right to obtain access, control others' access to their child's school records, participate on special education advisory committees, and exercise all the rights and privileges of IDEA to benefit their child. Additionally, IDEA validates the role of parents as educational decision makers for their child and encourages collaboration between parents and professionals (Harry, 2008; Pruitt, Wandry, & Hollums, 1998). In terms of parents being involved in the development and implementation of the IEP, an earlier study conducted by Lynch and Stein (1982) found that the majority of parents stated that they were involved in the development of their children's IEPs. However, based on the parent answers to the questions, the study revealed that the involvement consisted of parents simply attending the meetings and the teachers making all the decisions. They did not offer ideas for the IEPs. Similarly, a classic study by McKinney and Hocutt (1982) revealed that parents were not involved in the IEP process and could not recall the components of the IEP. These findings suggested that although parents perceive they are involved, the perceptions may not be based on a thorough understanding of the content and procedures employed in special education (see Green & Shinn, 1994). A 2014 study yielded similar results when it examined parents within two contexts: involvement at home for early intervention, and involvement at a center for early intervention. The results of the study revealed that practitioners are not meeting IDEA's goal of parents being active participants. Parents are not participating in a manner that is likely to have capacity building consequences and characteristics (Dunst, Bruder, & Espe-Sherwindt, 2014).

Likewise, African American parents of students with disabilities express frustration and anger at policies they believe prevent them from participating in their child's education (Brandon, 2007). Jacqueline Jordan Irvine (1990), in her classic book, *Black Students and School Failure: Policies, Practices, and Prescriptions*, argued that supports for parental involvement are a part of the hidden curriculum and descriptive practice that harms African American children. Much of the literature on parental involvement such as the classic studies of Lynch and Stein (1982) suggested African American parents are disinterested in their children's education and significantly less involved in education than their White counterparts. However, the foundational beliefs about education and its importance within the African American community is long standing. Other studies (e.g., Harry, 1992) have shown that these substantial differences between White and African American parents are a result of parents feeling alienated from schools, lacking knowledge about their rights as parents, feelings of mistrust toward school officials, encountering stressful life circumstances, and disapproval of the special education classifications.

BENEFITS OF PARENTAL ENGAGEMENT

Parent involvement in home–school collaboration helps to facilitate better educational outcomes for students. This collaboration includes CLD families. Home–school collaboration involves an exchange of communication between school officials and parents, which results in a shared responsibility among parents and educators and ultimately produces constructive results for students (Raffaele & Knoff, 1999). The 2001 No Child

Left Behind Act granted parents the power to make decisions in their children's education (Howard & Reynolds, 2008). This push for more parental involvement resulted from earlier research that illuminated the educational outcomes for students whose parents are involved. To counter these barriers, Wagner et al. (2003) contended that there must be a trusting and caring relationship between staff and families in order to engage families in the development of their children. Parent self-responsibility reflects parental engagement, which also reveals the behavior and attitudes of parents, their parenting styles, and the perceptions of their children (Wang, 2009).

Lazar, Broderick, Mastrilli, and Slostad (1999) found a positive relationship between parent involvement and a host of outcomes for students such as higher grades, long-term academic achievement, increases in student attendance, and enhanced motivation and self-esteem. Extensive evidence indicates that children whose parents are more involved in school show higher academic performance, and that such involvement contributes to children's achievement, attitudes and aspirations, even beyond the effects of family socioeconomic status and student ability (see Lazar et al., 1999). Through family–school links, African American families socialize their children by promoting expectations for success and increasing their children's likelihood of performing well in school. Bergman and Rogers (2016) reported that when parents are empowered with timely, and actionable information, student achievement increases. In their study, Bergman and Rogers (2016) noted that schools used text messages as a method for communicating with parents, resulting in a 1.1 percentage point increase in grades.

The literature is clear that parental involvement leads to greater academic success for students. However, White middle class values are used to define parent involvement (Lareau, 2000), thus excluding the determinations and of CLD groups all together. Thompson (2003a) surveyed 129 African American parents of secondary students on how they assisted their children in school. Selections revealed that parents who rated their involvement as excellent, were parents who from time to time (a) had conversations with teachers, (b) had students with few to zero suspensions, (c) had students who had higher scores in math and reading, (d) assisted at times with homework, (e) had students check for accuracy of work, (f) had students who had limited TV viewing, (g) bought books for their children, and (h) encouraged their children to go to college. Conversely, these parents were not parent volunteers in the classroom. They did not participate in all school activities, but they engaged in more behind the scenes or out of school activities with their students. These parents were empowered and engaged in the lives of their students; and they were responsible in the education of their students. Harry and Klingner (2006) maintained that based on their study, African American parents' ways of caring and their sources of pride were not always consistent with what schools considered important. However, the parents made efforts to fulfill what they perceived to be their responsibilities.

TRANSITIONING THROUGH THE SCHOOL YEARS

Parent involvement and the collaboration between teachers and parents differ from early-childhood/Head Start to kindergarten through middle school and high school. Policy makers, educators, and researchers (e.g., Obiakor, 2001; Obiakor, Grant, & Dooley, 2002) agree that family–school partnerships enhance children's educational experience and that their relationships are important as children transition from preschool to kindergarten. Transitioning from early childhood special education programs to public school kindergartens presents changes for children's families. This transition involves relinquishing ties with the familiar preschool setting, and adjusting to a school that may provide fewer opportunities for family involvement, yet place challenging academic and social demands on the child (Fowler, Schwartz, & Atwater, 1991). The transitions continue throughout students' educational journey from early childhood through high school and beyond.

Kindergarten and Elementary Years

Kindergarten constitutes children's first experience with formal schooling, and researchers such as Rimm-Kaufmann and Pianta (1999) demonstrated that supportive family relationships could help children negotiate cultural and academic discontinuities upon school entry. Family–school partnerships in kindergarten establish shared responsibilities of families and schools for children's education. In addition, such partnerships introduce families to school culture and buffer stress by offering stability while teacher, children, and curricula are changing.

Elementary schools are more likely than preschools to emphasize teacher professionalism. As a result, parents may perceive a greater social distance between them and their child's teacher and may feel less comfortable getting involved. Parents may exercise less freedom to choose their child's kindergarten compared to preschool. This usually affects parents' perceptions of how welcomed they are to participate in their child's school (see Rimm-Kaufmann & Pianta, 1999).

IMPLICATIONS FOR PRACTITIONERS

Embracing parent–professional relationships and family centered practices leads to family satisfaction with schools (Mahmood, 2013), and family satisfaction with schools occurs only within welcoming environments where there is trust, safety, fairness, and respect (Grace & Harrington, 2015). When parents know their voices are heard, and their decisions in the IEP development are considered and implemented, they are more likely to serve as active participants (McCloskey, 2010). The most effective collaborations occur when there are varied opportunities for partnerships for parents throughout the special education process (Thorp, 1997). Principles underlying successful partnership programs include a no-fault model where blame is not attributed to the family or school. Emphasizing and appreciating the strengths and assets of individuals facilitates schools' understanding the non-deficit approach of parental and family engagement. Schools must accent the importance of empowerment where families are actively involved in decision-making and choices for their personal lives. Moreover, it is highly suggested that schools utilize an ecological approach where there is recognition that the school context influences the family and the family influences the school (Rimm-Kaufmann & Pianta, 1999). Recognizing and grasping the meaningful approaches to learning that children hold when they arrive to school are beneficial to both schools and families (Adair, 2010).

Garcia and Hassan (2004) suggested family centered education initiatives not only advance the success of students, but also empower the parents as well. Their recommendation is for schools to "systematically plan, implement, and evaluate the various programmatic components that comprise the total educational process" (p. 114). Garcia and Hassan (2004) noted that when establishing a systematic approach to the program design, the program must be viewed as a set of "interrelated components which must be skillfully balanced." School leaders and administrators play critical roles in the special education process. They have considerable influence over the school organization in the areas of budget, climate, and leadership (Obiakor et al., 2010). Principals must hold the capacity to foster, maintain, and exemplify trusting relationships with all parents within the school (Sheldon, Angell, Stoner, & Roseland, 2010).

Koch (2016) summarized the need for schools to be conscious of (a) communicating with parents about their child's academic programming, whether it is disability related or not; (b) initiating communication, not just responding to parent-initiated communication; and (c) encouraging parent participation in school.

CONCLUSION

When parents feel involved and as a part of their child's academic program, their satisfaction with the school increases. Clearly, schools applying the above-mentioned suggestions are sure to empower parents as well as meet the parental involvement laws set forth by IDEA. Classroom teachers and educational leaders must about-face their commitment to properly preparing all students to participate in a democratic society (Beachum, 2011). Readjustments in school-based strategies that empower parents of young, atypical learners cannot occur in the absence of parents' voices. The two entities formulating a true partnership, grounded in trust, and mutual respect will surely produce maximum benefits for learners.

REFERENCES

Adair, J. K. (2010). *Ethnographic knowledge for early childhood.* Retrieved from http://files.eric.ed.gov/fulltext/ED511898.pdf

Adams, G., & McDaniel, M. (2012). *Barriers and opportunities: Helping smaller immigrant communities access the Illinois preschool for all program: Summary findings from three studies.* Washington, DC: Urban Institute.

Adentwi, I. K. (2005). *Curriculum development: An introduction.* Kumasi, Ghana: Skies Press.

Beachum, F. D. (2011). Culturally relevant leadership for complex 21st-century schools context. In *The Sage handbook of educational leadership* (pp. 26–34.) doi:10.4135/9781412980036.n3.

Bempechat, J. (1992). The role of parent involvement in children's academic achievement. *The School Community Journal, 82*(2), 85–102.

Bergman, P., & Rogers, T. (2016). Parent adoption of school communications technology: A 12-school experiment of default enrollment policies. *Society for Research on Educational Effectiveness.* Retrieved from http://files.eric.ed.gov/fulltext/ED567596.pdf

Brandon, R. R. (2007). African American parents: Improving connections with their child's educational environments. *Intervention in School and Clinic, 43*(2), 116–120.

Cardona, B., Sachin, J., & Canfield-Davis, K. (2012). Home-school relationships: A qualitative study with diverse families. *The Qualitative Report, 17*(70), 1–20.

Children Now. (2014). *Policy brief: Early childhood home visiting in California: The right place at the right time.* Retrieved from childrennow.org

Christmon, K. (1990). Parental responsibility of African American unwed adolescent fathers. *Adolescence, 25*(99), 645–653.

Clark, R. (1983). *Family life and school achievement: Why poor African American children succeed or fail.* Chicago, IL: The University of Chicago Press.

Comer, J. P., & Haynes, N. M. (1991). Parent involvement in schools: An ecological approach. *The Elementary School Journal, 91*(3), 271–277.

Dunst, C. J., Bruder, M., & Espe-Sherwindt, M. (2014). Family capacity-building in early childhood intervention: Do context and setting matter? *School Community Journal, 24*(1), 37–48.

Eekelaar, J. (1994). The interests of the child and the child's wishes: The role of dynamic self determination. *International Journal of Law and the Family, 8*(1), 42–61.

Epps, E. G. (1995). Race, class, and educational opportunity: Trends in the sociology of education. *Sociological Forum, 10*(4), 593–608.

Faerstein, L. (1981). Stress and coping in families of learning disabled children: A literature review. *Journal of Learning Disabilities, 14*(7), 420–424.

Fareo, D. O. (2015). Counseling intervention for family security. *Journal of Education and Practice, 6*(10), 64–69.

Fowler, S. A., Schwartz, I., & Atwater, J. (1991). Perspectives on the transition from preschool to kindergarten for children with disabilities and their families. *Exceptional Children, 58*(2), 136–141.

Frabutt, J. M., & Waldron, R. (2013). Reaching the youngest hearts and minds: Interviews with Diocesan leaders regarding Catholic early childhood education. *Catholic Education: A Journal of Inquiry and Practice, 17*(1/2), 4–40.

Garcia, D. C., & Hasson, D. J. (2004). Linguistically and culturally diverse populations: Key elements to consider. *School Community Journal, 14*(1), 113–137.

Grace, R. A., & Harrington, S. Y. (2015). Our children, our schools: Seeking solutions for improving the climate in urban public schools. *The Alabama Journal of Educational Leadership, 2*(1), 1–14.

Green, S. K., & Shinn, M. R. (1994). Parent attitudes about special education and reintegration: What is the role of student outcomes? *Exceptional Children, 61*(3), 269–272.

Grolnick, W. S., & Slowiaczek, M. L. (1994). Parents' involvement in children's schooling: A multidimensional conceptualization and motivational model. *Child Development, 65,* 237–252.

Harry, B. (1992). Restructuring the participation of African-American parents in special education. *Exceptional Children, 59*(2), 123–127.

Harry, B. (2008). Collaboration with culturally and linguistically diverse families: Ideal versus reality. *Exceptional Children, 74*(3), 372–388.

Harry, B., & Klingner, J. (2006). *Why are so many minority students in special education? Understanding race and disability in schools.* New York, NY: Teachers College Press.

Henderson, A. T., & Mapp, K. L. (2002). *A new wave of evidence: The impact of school, family, and community connections on student achievement.* Austin, TX: Southwest Educational Development Laboratory.

Hill, N. E., & Craft, S. A. (2003). Parent–school involvement and school performance: Mediated pathways among socioeconomically comparable African American and Euro-American families. *Journal of Educational Psychology, 93*(1), 74–83.

Howard, T. C., & Reynolds, R. (2008). Examining parent involvement of African American student in middle-class schools. *Educational Foundations, 22*(1–2), 79–98.

Irvine, J. J. (1990). *Black students and school failure: Policies, practices, and prescriptions.* Westport, CT: Greenwood.

Koch, K. (2016). The influence of parenting experience on special education teachers' pedagogy. *International Journal of Special Education, 31*(3), 1–19. Retrieved from http://files.eric.ed.gov/fulltext/EJ1120684.pdf

Lareau, A. (2000). *Home advantage: Social class and parental intervention in elementary education.* Lanham, MD: Rowman and Littlefield.

Lazar, A., Broderick, P., Mastrilli, T., & Slostad, F. (1999, Spring). Educating teachers for parent involvement. *Contemporary Education, 70*(3), 5–9.

Lehman, C. W. (2017). Early childhood: Language and bullying in an English medium school in China. *The Electronic Journal for English as a Second Language 21*(1), 1–14.

Lynch, E. W., & Stein, R. (1982). Perspectives on parent participation in special education. *Exceptional Education Quarterly, 3*(2), 56–63.

Mahmood, S. (2013). First-year preschool and kindergarten teachers: Challenges of working with parents. *School Community Journal, 23*(2), 55–86.

McCloskey, E. (2010). What do I know? Parental positioning in special education. *International Journal of Special Education, 25*(1), 162–170.

McKinney, J. D., & Hocutt, A. M. (1982). Public school involvement of parents of learning disabled and average achievers. *Exceptional Education Quarterly, 3*(2), 64–73.

National Association for the Education of Young Children. (2009). *Where we stand on responding to linguistic and cultural diversity.* Retrieved from http://www.naeyc.org/files/naeyc/file/positions/diversity.pdf

Ntumi, S. (2016). Challenges pre-school teachers face in the implementation of the early childhood curriculum in the cape coast metropolis. *Journal of Education and Practice, 7*(1), 54–62.

Obiakor, F. E. (2001). *It even happens in good schools: Responding to cultural diversity in today's classroom.* Thousand Oaks, CA: Corwin.

Obiakor, F. E., Grant, P., & Dooley, E. (2002). *Educating all learners: Refocusing the comprehensive support model.* Springfield, IL: Charles C. Thomas.

Obiakor, F. E., Harris, M. K., & Beachum, F. D. (2009). The state of special education for African American learners in Milwaukee. In G. L. Williams & F. E. Obiakor (Eds.), *The state of education of urban learners and possible solutions. The Milwaukee experience* (pp. 31–48). Dubuque, IA: Kendall Hunt.

Obiakor, F. E., Harris, M. K., Offor, M. T., & Beachum, F. D. (2010). African American learners in special education: A closer look at Milwaukee. *Multicultural Learning and Teaching, 5*(2), 28–48.

Office of Head Start. (2008). *Revisiting and updating the multicultural principle for Head Start programs serving children ages birth to five.* Retrieved from https://eclkc.ohs.acf.hhs.gov/sites/default/files/pdf/principles-01-10-revisiting-multicultural-principles-hs-english_0.pdf

Pomerantz, E. M., Moorman, E. A., & Litwack, S. D. (2007). The how, whom, and why of parents' engagement in children's schooling: More is not necessarily better. *Review of Educational Research, 77*(3), 373–410.

Pruitt, P., Wandry, D., & Hulloms, D. (1998). Listen to us! Parents speak out about their interactions with special educators. *Preventing School Failure, 42*(4),161–170.

Raffaele, M., & Knoff, L. M. (1999). Improving home-school collaboration with disadvantaged families. *School Psychology Review, 28*(3), 448–468.

Rimm-Kaufman, S. E., & Pianta, R. C. (1999). Patterns of family-school contact in preschool and kindergarten. *School Psychology Review, 28*(3), 426–440.

Sheldon, D. L., Angell, M. E., Stoner, J. B., & Roseland, B. D. (2010). School principals' influence on trust: Perspectives of mothers of children with disabilities. *The Journal of Educational Research, 103*(3), 159–170.

Squelch, J. (2006). Back to school for parents: Implementing responsible parenting agreements and orders in Western Australia. *Education and the Law, 18*(4), 247– 266.

Thompson, G. L. (2003a). *What African American parents want educators to know.* Westport, CT: Praeger.

Thorp, E. (1997). Increasing opportunities for partnership with culturally and linguistically diverse families. *Intervention in School & Clinic, 32*(5), 261–268.

Wagner, M., Spiker, D., Lynn, M., Gerlach-Downie, S., & Hernandez, F. (2003). Dimensions of parental engagement in home visiting programs: Exploratory study. *Topics in Early Childhood Special Education, 23*(4), 171–183.

Wang, M. T. (2009). School climate support for behavioral and psychological adjustment: Testing the mediating effect of social competence. *School Psychology Quarterly, 24*(4), 240–251.

CHAPTER 7

SCHOOL–COMMUNITY PARTNERSHIPS

Educating Young Children

Bridgie A. Ford, Shernavaz Vakil, and Lynn S. Kline

The essentiality of school–community partnerships in maximizing educational opportunities for students is evident from the vast directives embedded within federal mandates, professional standards for teachers and administrators, parent and community organizations, and advocacy groups. Despite the evidence supporting the impact of school–community partnerships on educational outcomes for students and school facilities, school districts often manifest policies and practices that inhibit the collaboration with significant professional and informal community resources that provide valuable services to the increasing percentages of families (and their children) from culturally and linguistically diverse (CLD) backgrounds. Given the importance of partnerships and student outcomes, the fundamental concepts addressed in this chapter are, community organizations, school–community partnerships, and school–community partnerships. Additionally, we propose the incorporation of Ford's (2004) Three Phase Model for Preparing Educators for School Partnerships with Significant Multicultural Community Resources (SMCR) to assist school

Educating Young Children With and Without Exceptionalities, pages 91–104
Copyright © 2019 by Information Age Publishing
All rights of reproduction in any form reserved.

personnel to effectively connect with significant multicultural community organizations/agencies. The elements of intention, collaboration, communication, and trust are embedded throughout the process of establishing productive relations between school and multicultural community organizations.

A CASE IN POINT

During a class discussion a graduate student employed as a paraprofessional, enrolled in a special education course taught by one of the authors shared concerns that she and her co-teachers in a local "community learning center" school setting were experiencing regarding the behavior exhibited by one of the second graders, an African American male, with special needs classified as having specific learning disabilities. The paraprofessional described the daily struggles they experienced as they attempted to address the targeted student's externalizing behaviors (i.e., impulsivity, oppositional, and misconduct). Despite the student's aggressive behavior, they liked him, because at times, he was cooperative and he was liked by most of the other students, even though his outbursts frightened them. The co-teachers were very concerned because the legal guardians, the grandparents, rejected the school's recommendation to seek family counseling services offered by a local agency used by the school district. The paraprofessional reported that there was talk about moving the student to a full-time self-contained setting; however, the co-instructional team worried that this move could increase the externalizing behavior and result in the student eventually dropping out of high school and/or ending up in the juvenile court system. In response to the course instructor's inquiry, as to the reasons the grandparents shared for not seeking the recommended family counseling, the paraprofessional explained that the grandparents said their grandson was not "mentally ill," that he was a good boy who helped out around the house; he just had problems handling himself when he became frustrated. The grandfather did not want to talk about their family business with strangers and feared going to counseling would result in having their grandson taken away from them. The instructor asked the paraprofessional how the recommended counseling agency was selected. The paraprofessional reported that it was the counseling agency listed on the district's approved list of professional community resources. At this point, the instructor asked if the school used the professional services of the local agency, Minority Behavioral Counseling Group, that specialized in working with African-American and Latino families and school-age youth, especially males. The paraprofessional admitted that she was not familiar with the agency but she would ask the co-teachers. During the next class meeting, the paraprofessional shared that the teaching team was not familiar with that particular agency because it was not on the school's recommended list but, the school counselor was aware of the agency and planned to share information about the agency with the grandparents emphasizing the agency's expertise and success in working with African American families.

The "Case in Point" illustrates a critical issue too often embedded in school district policy and practice that demand examination. In order to access quality services for all students in today's highly diverse schools, school personnel must expand their resources to include formal and informal community organizations/agencies that specialize in services to families from CLD backgrounds. The targeted urban school district described in this case had recently renovated and renamed many of the school buildings Community Learning Centers to embrace a school–community partnership framework. The district's acknowledgment and endorsement of select agencies and its non-usage or underutilization of others, is in direct conflict with the school-community framework it is seeking to establish. By building relationships with both traditional, familiar public service organizations, and those formal and informal community entities (i.e., organizations/agencies/individuals) valued by diverse families, schools broaden their reach and promote student learning (Blank & Shah, 2004; Ford, 2004).

School–community partnerships vary in type and degree. Terms such as community schools, integrated, collaborative, coordinated, school linked services, full service community schools, and 21st century schools are used to describe program models that reflect the present focus on collaborating with community agencies and organizations to enhance educational attainment (Dryfoos, 2002; Ford, 2004; Rigsby, 1995). As emphasized in the Individuals With Disabilities Education Act (IDEA; 2004) legislative mandates for students with disabilities and for all students in the Every Student Succeeds Act (ESSA; 2016), this current "linking of resources" is endorsed and conceived as vital in the provision of quality educational services to meet the needs of all students, pre-K–12. A school–community partnership encompasses two interrelated premises. First, when working with students of all ages, (pre-K–12), it is essential that schools seek the engagement of community organizations and agencies and the involvement of significant others (i.e., parents/families). And second, the realization that schools alone cannot adequately address the multifaceted problems confronted by today's students (with and without disabilities) and the often disconnect between school personnel and students from diverse backgrounds (e.g., culturally and/or linguistically different) makes school–community partners absolute. These realities are more pronounced for districts in urban, rural, and low socioeconomic locales where the prevalent contributing issues often include but are not limited to poverty, poor health, hunger, unemployment, and teen pregnancy. These out-of-school, non-educational predicaments serve as barriers to students' academic achievement and must be appropriately addressed through collaborative school–community networks. In the education of young children, researchers (Epstein & Salina, 2004; Henderson & Mapp, 2002; Sheldon, 2003; Dunst, 2000) recognize that a well-organized program of family and community partnerships yields many benefits for schools and their students. Henderson and Mapp (2002) documented that connections to community groups can expand the resources available to schools for both staff and families to improve facilities, secure more funding, enhance academic programs, improve social and health services, and provide new after-school programs. Through school–family–community partnerships, teachers are challenged to establish authentic bonds with significant formal and informal community entities (organizations/agencies, individuals) that empower families and enable them to better advocate for their children educationally as well as provide them with valuable services (Epstein, 2010; Ford, 2004).

COMMUNITY ORGANIZATIONS

Of the many changes that have shaped the field of early childhood, one salient issue now recognized is that family, community organizations which support them, and education are inseparable dimensions (Voss & Bufkin, 2011). Young children are embedded within the context of community and family and cannot be separated from it. Therefore, most effective early childhood programs are family centered, where the community and family are an integral part of the program. Early childhood programs which embrace the culture of families and the communities which support them are inclusive and are more likely to have a greater impact on the development of the child (Grant & Ray, 2012). Because communities play dominant roles in students' educational advancement, infrequent contact in students' communities and connections with significant community organizations/agencies/individuals by school personnel is viewed as opportunities lost to positively affect educational performance and hence, intensifies inequities (Nieto, 1992). School–community involvement as a strategy to strengthen educational attainment is not a new phenomenon or educational reform movement. The civil rights and social reform movements during the 1960s saw the emergence of alternative social programs and community empowerment education spearheaded by minority groups and communities (e.g., African-American and Latino). This was in reaction to failing schools. However, it was the combination of alarming educational achievement reports during the 1980s (e.g., *A Nation At-Risk* by the National Commission on Excellence in Education, 1983), declining fiscal resources in the 1990s, and the spilling over of out-of-school problems by students (e.g., poverty and inadequate health care) that magnified educational problems. The dire situation moved school officials to assume more accountability (not just minority parents, professional and community organizations) for transitioning into a school–community paradigm. Fiscally and educationally, it became important to institute collaborative models of school–community networks. School personnel usually possess knowledge of and firsthand experiences with certain categories of public service organizations/agencies (e.g., medical and mental agencies, social services, and juvenile service; Ford, 2004). Congruent with federal education legislation, professional education standards, and research focusing on factors impacting educational outcomes, school districts' collaborative school–community partnerships must be conceptualized from a more comprehensive framework to promote quality services for young children.

Additionally, a critical phenomenon impacting schools today is the changing demographics within the student populations which are becoming increasingly culturally and linguistically diverse. Schools in the United States are often the first point of contact for children from immigrant families as they acculturate into American society (Stufft & Brogadir, 2011); and engaging with families strengthens the cultural competency of teachers with a positive impact on English language learners (ELLs; Díaz-Rico, 2013). Crucial then are school connections to culturally based community organizations/agencies that support the success of young children. These connections must become part of the school's framework. Teachers must form the primary interactions when engaging with families and their young children and serve as ongoing sources of information for families. Through school–community partnerships, teachers are better able to obtain authentic knowledge about families, and share information about relevant community resources based on the needs of young children and their families. Teacher preparation and district in-service programs however, have failed to equip teacher candidates and practicing teachers respectively with the framework regarding the value of school–community partnerships, and the knowledge, skills, and attitudes required to engage in them (Ford, Stuart, & Vakil, 2015). As observed in the opening "Case in Point," rather than collaborating with community organizations and resources which best fit the needs of the student and family, the teaching team referred to sources identified on a standard list. This was further exacerbated by (a) the district's exclusion of relevant community organizations, and (b) the reluctance of the team to seek other available options despite the grandparents' refusal to participate in the one selected by the school. Additionally, the "Case in Point" also serves as evidence of why CLD families with young children who have special needs and are in need of counseling as a related service may underutilize mental health services. Culturally competent school personnel would have an awareness of relevant community resources, advocate for those to be included on the district's recommended list, and would know how to address the grandfather's realistic concerns about traditional mental health services.

TYPES OF COMMUNITY ORGANIZATIONS

Speer and Perkins (2002) explained that categorizing community organizations is difficult, because they may range from voluntary organizations to professional service agencies to informal groups. These organizations are often considered to include churches, unions, schools, health care agencies, social-service groups, fraternities, and clubs. Community organizations are predominantly conceptualized as nonprofit, but broader conceptions of community sometimes include all organizations, including for-profit enterprises. Speer and Perkins (2002) further report that service agencies are frequently termed *community-based* agencies because their service has shifted from centralized institutional settings to dispersed geographical locations, providing greater access to residents. This chapter discusses both formal and informal organizations and categorizes them as either *traditional* or *significant multicultural community resources* (SMCR; Ford, 2002, 2004, 2006).

We refer to *formal community organization/agencies* as

1. traditional professional public service organizations (e.g., medical agencies, social services, juvenile services, counseling, etc.); or
2. significant multicultural community resources (SMCR)—professional organizations that specialize in working with families from CLD populations.

They are primarily located in diverse neighborhoods and communities and local community residents perceive them as providing valuable *significant* services (see Ford, 2002, 2004, 2006).

Informal organizations include:

1. Profit and not-for-profit organizations/agencies in general (they are churches, unions, social-service groups, fraternities, social clubs, agencies, and neighborhood associations/block clubs individuals); or
2. significant multicultural community resources (SMCR). They are profit and not-for-profit service or social organizations, sororities, fraternities, clubs or agencies, religious group/churches, neighborhood associations/block clubs and individuals that specialize in working with families from CLD populations are primarily located in diverse neighborhoods and communities and local community residents perceive them as providing valuable *significant* services (see Ford, 2002, 2004).

Garcia (1991) and Blank and Shah (2004) noted that public schools are and should be a community affair. For example, Garcia (1991) expounded that the school's community consists of varied social groups which interact with each other, developing cooperative and interdependent networks of relationships. However, schools are more likely to extend and participate in the important cooperative and interdependent networks with social groups which are not poor or from multicultural backgrounds. When schools engage in school–community partnerships, Sanders (2001) revealed that they *underutilize* community partners such as faith based organizations (e.g., churches), volunteer organizations, community-based organizations (e.g., sororities, fraternities, and neighborhood associations), and individuals in the school community volunteering their time, energy, and talents. As highlighted above, SMCR services may include educational, counseling, advocacy, financial, legal, and empowerment supports. SMCR services may also impact the overall well-being of the school and various developmental needs of students. For example, within many segments of the African American community, the African American church remains an important leadership institution (Billinsley & Caldwell, 1991). It extends a host of outreach programs to support educational (e.g., early childhood and literacy programs) initiatives.

Casas and Furlong (1994) and Rueda (1997) described some examples of innovative community-based programs that have made efforts to enhance the quality of Latino parent participation. These examples include Fiesta Educativa, the Say Yes to a Youngster's Future, the MALDEF Parent Leadership Program, and the Parent Empowerment Program-Students Included/Padres en Poder-Si (PEP-si). Also, as the number of refugees entering the United States increases, community organizations such as the International Institute, American Red Cross, and faith-based programs are collaborating with schools to support and provide services to young children and families who are displaced (Dustmann et al., 2017). In many cities, community resources that target the needs of American Indians may be centralized or confined into a local or regional "Indian center." Many years ago, Moll, Amanti, Neff, and Gonzalez (1992) used the term *funds of knowledge* to refer to historically accumulated and culturally developed bodies of knowledge and skills essential for household or individual functioning and well-being. In their work, they focus on preparing teachers to obtain and use household information regarding Mexican and Yaqui families and communities' funds of knowledge. Moll et al. (1992) concluded that an awareness and incorporation of the student's household and community funds of knowledge can help educators draw on the resources outside the context of the classroom. In the same view, Blank and Shah (2004) emphasizes that local community organizations provide a common ground for residents to share problems and resources. Organizations thus serve to mediate between seemingly powerless individuals or families and the large institutions (i.e., schools) of mass society.

Finally, many families from CLD backgrounds have a history of negative experiences with and mistrust of the school. Differences in income, language, dialects, values and belief systems, or insensitivity to religious beliefs impact involvement of multicultural families and communities with the school. Consequently, families are reluctant and/or intimidated to take advantage of their legal rights (Banks, 2004; Cummins, 1986; Harry, 2008). For those families, a "neutral" mechanism is needed to empower them with information and skills to advocate for their young children. Formal and/or informal SMCR may be used as a strategy to promote increased family involvement with schools. Since SMCR are essential elements of many multicultural communities, broader usage, rather than underutilization is needed.

SCHOOL–COMMUNITY PARTNERSHIPS

Effective school, family, and community involvement recognizes the social and human capital that families and communities bring to the table. While human capital addresses the knowledge and skills families and organizations bring to meetings, social capital emphasizes building relationships between participating schools, families, and community organizations. Social capital relies on trust between these stakeholders. Strong interactions between schools and communities provide coordinated resources for families (Coleman, 1991). Schools and community organizations should collaborate to find common areas of service to build on so that goals of community organizations align with contributions to school goals (Davis, 2000). Following are specific elements that could build productive school–community partnerships.

Intention

Community based organizations providing services for young children with disabilities must be purposeful and deliberate in their efforts to enhance learning and development. While community organizations bring their expertise to the team, to be effective, schools should communicate a unifying purpose which is achievable, concrete, measurable, and understood by all. A unifying document may help guide the collaboration efforts between agencies to optimize opportunities (Friend & Cook, 2016). It is critical to understanding that the early years are when children develop most rapidly. With the advancement of technology and research in the field of education, community organizations providing services to young children must be flexible enough to keep up with the rapid changes in the field and adapt to new research and legislative requirements. Additionally, it is critical that services be provided where they are most needed and easily accessible to families (Davis, 2000).

Collaboration

While schools are the lead institutions charged with educating young children, community entities are able to provide support or related services. When schools collaborate with community entities including public services, businesses, cultural organizations, and other groups to share responsibility for children's education and development, it enhances the educational outcomes for all young children (Ford, 2012; Epstein & Salinas, 2004). Clearly, collaboration can be difficult and challenging. Through authentic collaboration between schools and community entities the focus shifts from solely compliance to meaningful outcomes. The emphasis on shared accountability of outcomes should guide school community partnerships. However, shared accountability does not negate the primary accountability of schools for their actions (Friend & Cook, 2017).

Communication

The need for integrating services has received a lot of attention, and there has been little focus on the deteriorating communication and team processes required to effectively collaborate when meeting the needs of diverse children (Wright, Stegelin, & Hartle, 2007; Grant & Ray, 2012). Epstein (2010) stated that while school personnel, community organizations, and families care about the student success, and want to collaborate, they often struggle to build positive relationships; therefore, adversarial relationships often arise. As Epstein (2010) pointed out, a "rhetoric rut" in which educators talk about collaboration and partnerships but are unable to actually put these statements into action should be challenged.

Trust

While the belief that "all children can learn" should be fundamental and almost simplistic, this concept is far more complex when applied to the diverse range of characteristics and abilities enrolled in schools today. Too often, school personnel and formal community entities operate from a deficit framework which stokes distrust between families, schools, and community entities (Allen & Cowdery, 2015; Welton & Vakil, 2010). In order to build trust in school community partnerships, the focus must be on valuing the different expertise and resources available in school and community.

ROLE OF TEACHER PREPARATION PROGRAMS

In his classical work, Cummins (1986) concluded that the major reason previous attempts at educational reform have been unsuccessful is that the relationships between teachers and students and between schools and communities have remained essentially unchanged. Therefore, preparing school personnel with knowledge of and skills to engage with organizations/agencies most familiar to school districts and SMCR community-based organizations is required to maximize educational opportunities for all young children (Banks, 2004; Comer, 1980; Ford, 2004; Ford et al., 2015; Ladson-Billings, 1995). As noted in the opening "Case in Point," the co-teachers' lack of awareness of SMCR serves as a barrier to effective communication with the grandparents. If SMCR are to be systematically infused within school–community partnerships and used to impact outcomes for CLD students, there must be corresponding changes in knowledge, skills, and attitudes of school personnel. Teacher preparation programs must expose teacher candidates to coursework and hands-on experiences that focus on

- evaluating personal frameworks (e.g., biases, assumptions, attitudes, and lack of knowledge) about communities of the students they will serve;
- examining past and current school-linkages with SMCR of local districts;
- communicating effectively and consistently with SMCR;
- sharing information about SMCR with other professionals through building level teams activities;
- sharing information with families about relevant SMCR;
- incorporating and utilizing knowledge about SMCR into the school climate to enhance educational goals; and
- documenting the impact of students' involvement in SMCR programming.

ESTABLISHING COMPREHENSIVE
SCHOOL–COMMUNITY PARTNERSHIPS

Ford's (2004) three phase model for preparing educators for school community partnerships is an adapted framework that creates a Comprehensive School–Community Partnership: Culturally Responsive model (Ford, 2004). While the adapted model includes community organizations/agencies in general, the emphasis is on SMCR entities which traditionally are marginalized as valuable resources. The elements of intention, collaboration, communication, and trust should be interwoven throughout the process of establishing productive school–community partnerships. See Figure 7.1.

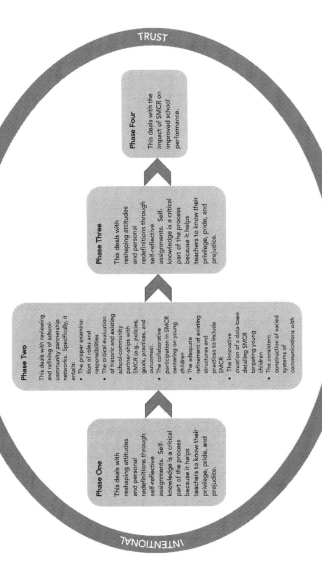

Figure 7.1

CONCLUSION

In this chapter, we have operated under the assertion that school–community partnerships are (a) crucial to student outcomes, and (b) to be broadened to include entities that respond to the needs of the diverse population of young children with and without disabilities and their families. The population in schools today is rapidly changing to include more CLD young children. Given the documented benefits of consultative partnerships for optimal student success, schools should be proactive in researching factors which influence school–community partnerships. Finally, we proposed a model adapted from Ford's (2004) three phase model for preparing educators for school–community partnerships as a contextual premise to establish and maintain comprehensive school–community networks.

REFERENCES

Allen, E. K., & Cowdery, G. E. (2015). *The exceptional child: Inclusion in early childhood education.* Albany, NY: Delmar.

Banks, C. A. M. (2004). Intercultural and intergroup education, 1929–1959: Linking schools and communities. In *Handbook of research on multicultural education* (pp. 753–769). San Francisco, CA: Jossey-Bass

Billingsley, A., & Caldwell, C. H. (1991). The church, the family, and the school in the African American community. *The Journal of Negro Education, 60*(3), 427–440.

Blank, M., & Shah, B. (2004). Educators and community sharing responsibility for student learning. *INFO Brief.* Retrieved from http://sparkaction.org/node/26370

Casas, J. M., & Furlong, M. J. (1994). School counselors as advocates for increased Hispanic parent participation in schools. In *Multicultural counseling in schools: A practical handbook* (pp. 121–155). London, England: Pearson.

Coleman, M. (2013). *Empowering family-teacher partnerships: Building connections within diverse communities.* Los Angeles, CA: SAGE.

Comer, J. P. (1980). *School power: Implications of an intervention project: With a new preface and epilogue.* New York, NY: Free Press.

Cummins, J. (1986). Empowering minority students: A framework for intervention. *Harvard Educational Review, 56*(1), 18–37.

Davis, D. (2000). *Supporting parent, family, and community involvement in your school.* Portland, OR: Northwest Regional Educational Laboratory.

Diaz-Rico, L. T. (2013). *The crosscultural, language, and academic development handbook: A complete k–12 reference guide.* London, England: Pearson.

Dryfoos, J. (2002). Partnering full-service community schools: Creating new institutions. *Phi Delta Kappan, 83*(5), 393–399.

Dunst, C. J. (2000). Revisiting "rethinking early intervention." *Topics in Early Childhood Education, 20*(2), 95–104.

Dustmann, C., Fasani, F., Frattini, T., Minale, L., & Schönberg, U. (2017). On the economics and politics of refugee migration. *Economic Policy, 32*(91), 497–550.

Epstein, J. L. (2010). *School, family, and community partnerships: Preparing educators and improving schools.* Boulder, CO: Westview Press.

Epstein, J. L., & Salinas, K. C. (2004). Partnering with families and communities. *Educational leadership, 61*(8), 12–19.

Ford, B. A. (2002). African American community resources: Essential education enhancers fro African American children and youth. In F. E. Obiakor & B. A. Ford (Eds.), *Creating successful learning environments for African American learners with exceptionalities* (pp. 159–173). Thousand Oaks, CA: Corwin Press.

Ford, B. A. (2004). Preparing special educators for culturally responsive school-community partnerships, *Teacher Education and Special Education, 27*(3), 224–230.

Ford, B. A. (2006). Culturally responsive school-community partnerships. In *White teachers/diverse classrooms* (pp. 286–300). Herndon, VA: Stylus.

Ford, B. A., Stuart, D., & Vakil, S. (2015). Culturally responsive teaching in the 21st century inclusive classroom. *Journal of the International Association of Special Education, 15*(2), 56–62.

Ford, D. Y. (2012). Culturally different students in special education: Looking backward to move forward. *Exceptional Children, 78*(4), 391–405.

Friend, M. P., & Cook, L. (2016). *Interactions: Collaboration skills for school professionals* (8th ed.). Boston, MA: Pearson Education.

Garcia, R. L. (1991). *Teaching in a pluralistic society: Concepts, models, strategies.* New York, NY: HarperCollins.

Grant, K. B., & Ray, J. A. (2018). *Home, school, and community collaboration: Culturally responsive family involvement* (4th ed.). Thousand Oaks, CA: SAGE.

Harry, B. (2008). Collaboration with culturally and linguistically diverse families: Ideal versus reality. *Exceptional Children, 74*(3), 372–388.

Henderson, A. T., & Mapp, K. L. (2002). A new wave of evidence: The impact of school, family, and community connections on student achievement. Annual synthesis 2002. In *National Center for Family and Community Connections with Schools.* Austin, TX: SEDL. Retrieved from http://www.sedl.org/connections/resources/evidence.pdf

Ladson-Billings, G. (1995). Toward a theory of culturally relevant pedagogy. *American educational research journal, 32*(3), 465–491.

Moll, L. C., Amanti, C., Neff, D., & Gonzalez, N. (1992). Funds of knowledge for teaching: Using a qualitative approach to connect homes and classrooms. *Theory Into Practice, 31*(2), 132–141.

National Commission on Excellence in Education. (1983). *A nation at risk: The imperative for educational reform.* Washington, DC: Author.

Nieto, S. (1992). *Affirming diversity: The sociopolitical context of multicultural education.* White Plains, NY: Longman.

Rigsby, L. C. (1995). Introduction: The need for new strategies. In *School/community connections* (pp. 1–18). San Francisco, CA: Jossey-Bass.

Rueda, R. (1997, November). Fiesta educativa: A community-based organization. Paper presented at Council for Exceptional Children Multicultural Symposium, New Orleans, LA.

Sanders, M. (2001). *New paradigm or old wine? The status of technology education practice in the United States.* Retrieved from http://scholar.lib.vt.edu/ejournals/JTE/v12n2/sanders.html

Sheldon, S. B. (2003). Linking school–family–community partnerships in urban elementary schools to student achievement on state tests. *Urban Review, 35*(2), 149–165.

Speer, P. W., & Perkins, D. D. (2002). Community-based organizations, agencies and groups. In J. Guthrie (Ed.) *Encyclopedia of education, 2nd ed.* (pp. 431–441). New York, NY: Macmillan Reference USA.

Stufft, D. L., & Brogadir, R. (2011). Urban principals' facilitation of English language learning in public schools. *Education and Urban Society, 43*(5), 560–575.

U.S. Department of Education. (2004). Individuals with Disabilities Education Act of 2004. Retrieved from http://idea.ed.gov

U.S. Department of Education. (2016, April 9). Every Student Succeeds Act (ESSA). Retrieved from http://www.ed.gov/essa?src=m

Voss, J. A., & Bufkin, L. J. (2011). Teaching all children: Preparing early childhood preservice teachers in inclusive settings. *Journal of Early Childhood Teacher Education, 32*(4), 338–354.

Welton, E., & Vakil, S. (2010). Enhancing the development of dispositions in preservice teacher preparation programs, *Journal of Psychology of the Romanian Academy, 56*(3–4), 261–268.

Wright, K., Stegelin, D. A., & Hartle, L. (2007). *Building family, school, and community partnerships.* Upper Saddle River, NJ: Prentice Hall.

CHAPTER 8

OPTIMIZING THE PHYSICAL AND MENTAL HEALTH OF YOUNG CHILDREN WITH AND WITHOUT EXCEPTIONALITIES

Eugene Asola and Sonya Sanderson

Physical activity and wellness has become an integral part of the lifelong healthy lifestyle of many people all over the world. Our current living and working conditions has exacerbated sedentary living created by the rapid advancement in technology and advancing economies. Consequently, changes in lifestyle and the demands and nature of our jobs have brought about tremendous stress and pressure on individuals and families. In a related fashion, the physical, social, mental, and educational needs of today's young children living under these technologically advanced conditions, brings with it many unintended consequences. These consequences include the lack of physical activity, affordable healthcare access, poverty, financial constraints, and many other health related diseases that all contribute to increasing mental health issues among young children with and without exceptionalities. Health and wellness, therefore, have become

Educating Young Children With and Without Exceptionalities, pages 105–118
Copyright © 2019 by Information Age Publishing
All rights of reproduction in any form reserved.

major concerns especially with the current obesity crisis among young and older Americans.

The constitution of the World Health Organization (WHO) defined health as "a state of complete physical, mental and social well-being and not merely the absence of disease or infirmity" (WHO, 2016a, p. 1). This organization emphasized that, "the enjoyment of the highest attainable standard of health is one of the fundamental rights of every human being without distinction of race, religion, and political belief, economic or social condition" (see WHO, 2016a, p. 1). Since healthy development of children is of basic importance, it is necessary for people who provide critical services to understand that, persons with mental illness can experience increased risk of physical illness such as coronary heart disease, diabetes, hypertension, stroke, and emphysema (Lambert, Velakolis, & Pantelis, 2003). Even though the benefits of physical activity for health and mental health is unquestionable (Penedo & Dahn, 2005), research shows that young children with physical and mental health (PMH) problems are likely to experience low levels of physical activity and become less physically active than those without (Osborn, Nazareth, & King, 2006). It is therefore important that health care providers and educators understand the issues associated with physical activity and mental health facing young children with or without exceptionalities. Understanding this point gives impetus to educational and health professionals in their ability to provide needed services for successful teaching and learning. As a result all healthy young children should be nurtured and supported to think and act responsibly in any given situation devoid of any mental or physical health challenges. It behooves us then, as educators and health care providers to create opportunities for young children to maintain "a sound mind" as a means of achieving a healthy body, free from disease or infirmity.

Over the past several years, physical inactivity and health related diseases have risen to an unprecedented level that warrants the attention and immediate action of health and education professionals, policy makers, and families. The consequence can be much more devastating within special populations, dealing with PMH issues and considering that young children with and without exceptionalities are vulnerable. For instance, the first mental health report by the Centers for Disease Control and Prevention (2013), "Mental Health Surveillance Among Children—United States, 2005–2011," described a grim picture of the number of U.S. children aged 3 to 17 years who were diagnosed with specific mental disorders between 2005 and 2011. The report showed that 6.8% had attention deficit hyperactivity disorder (ADHD); 3.5% behavioral or conduct problems; 3% anxiety; 1.1% autism spectrum disorder; and 0.2% Tourette among children aged 6 to 17 years. As presented, the report is evident and suggests a dire need for some action as an intervention to address the PMH of young children with and without exceptionalities. The question then is, "What can be done to optimize the PMH of young children?" This chapter answers this question.

PHYSICAL HEALTH OF YOUNG CHILDREN

Clay (2007) reiterated the 2002 study of the Health Resources and Services Administration. As Clay (2007) noted, "An estimated 5.2 million to 7.8 million children with a significant chronic health problem attend school every day in the United States" (p. 389). There is the need for some type of intervention programs to be established to address PMH issues among young children. This can be done and supported by stakeholders, health care service providers, and educators within the school environment. As the U.S. Census Bureau (2003) stated, the changing demographics in the United States implies the majority of children with mental health problems may be coming from an ethnic minority group or from families with low socioeconomic backgrounds within the next 2 decades. This trend may pose serious problems to some communities and families, if allowed to continue without intervention programs (see Clay, 2007). Undoubtedly, it is necessary for health care providers and educators to take into account cultural and socioeconomic variables related to health problems when providing health care and educational services to children (see Clay, 2007; Clay, Mordhorst, & Lehn, 2002; Shade, Kelly, & Oberg, 1997).

Asola and Obiakor (2016) emphasized that an in-depth understanding of how individual cultures influence their perspectives and behaviors and how they relatively affect student learning in schools can be handled better by a culturally competent and responsive leader. Health care service providers and educators may be considered leaders in their respective roles. They collaborate to provide the needed services to children with or without exceptionalities, especially in the educational sectors. The current trends and growth in diverse populations in the United States today presents tremendous challenges to leaders at all levels and therefore demands unique attention and opportunities to intervene. Health care providers and educators should endeavor to apply culturally responsive methods, as well as innovative intervention strategies to meet students' PMH needs. This may help minimize the negative stereotypes and feelings of isolation many PMH students experience in American educational institutions, including children of immigrants (Sofo, Nandzo, Asola, & Ajongba, 2013). A recent study by Carpenter-Song and Snell-Rood (2017) found that social changes and rising social inequality in the rural United States have affected the experience and meaning of mental illness and treatment seeking within rural communities. As established, rural Americans face serious mental health disparities, including higher rates of suicide and depression compared to residents in urban areas; and substance abuse rates in rural areas now equal those in urban areas. Despite these increased risks, people living in rural areas are less likely than their urban counterparts to seek or receive mental health services (Carpenter-Song & Snell-Rood, 2017). It is recommended that young children with PMH issues within these populations be given the necessary attention and care to ensure they function well in their educational environments.

The Centers for Disease Control and Prevention (CDC, 2017) recounted the report by the Surgeon General on Physical Activity and Health-Adolescents and Young Adults that noted that, nearly half of American youth aged 12 to 21 years are not vigorously active on a regular basis, and that only 19% of all high school students are physically active for 20 minutes or more per week. Studies show that regular physical activity can help people with chronic disabling conditions improve the stamina and muscle strength, as well as improve psychological well-being and quality of life (CDC, 2017). Sadly, persons with disabilities are less likely to engage in regular moderate to vigorous physical activity than persons without disabilities (CDC, n.d.). Presumably, as stated by Asola and Obiakor (2016), the incidence of learners with physical and health impairments prevails all over the world, but the frequency and rise in certain parts of the world can be exacerbated by several factors including wars, food and nutrition, diseases, medicines/pesticides, and the environment. The school, community, and health care institutions constitute the environment that may positively or negatively affect the state of students with PMH issues. These issues raise serious health concerns considering that PMH of young children has been paid little attention over the past decade or more. Children who have PMH issues need to be provided opportunities to promote their health and prevent unnecessary diseases. Parents, educational authorities, and mental health care providers must work together to promote and sustain good physical and mental health for all children, irrespective of their conditions.

Depending on the type of physical activity, duration, and intensity, physical activity appears to relieve symptoms of depression, anxiety, and improves mood (Guszkowska, 2004). Simple but important skills that may enhance good and acceptable behaviors, attitudes, and values that most children need to build interpersonal and social relations may be lacking in children with PMH. Their ability to perform basic daily tasks is challenged by self-awareness, leadership, teamwork, self-control, and motivation since these children lack these socio-emotional skills. Physical and mental health of young children with or without exceptionalities is therefore critical for overall health and well-being. Finding alternative methods to address this issue by way of interventions is as crucial as sustaining optimal health and wellness in young children. Optimizing the PMH of young children is an active process of creating awareness on how to make good choices towards a more successful healthy living. This is important because it involves the mind and body; and poor physical health can lead to an increased risk of developing mental health problems. Research shows that mental health problems affect 10%–20% of children and adolescents worldwide, accounting for 15%–30% of disability-adjusted life years (DALYs) lost during the first 3 decades of life (Kieling et al., 2011). Physical and mental health of young children with and without exceptionalities cannot be insulated from secondary occurring phenomenon. For example, the mental health foundation reports that one way that poor mental health can be detrimental to physical health is schizophrenia which in turn doubles the risk of death from heart disease, and three times the risk of death from respiratory disease. Sadly, it is true that people with mental health conditions are less likely to receive the physical healthcare they deserve, and also less likely to go for routine checks for blood pressure, weight, diabetes, and cholesterol, that may detect symptoms of poor health earlier.

Leas and McCabe (2007) identified several factors associated with lower levels of physical activity among people with mental illness to include (a) low education and socioeconomic status, (b) high body mass index, (c) ethnicity, (d) medical factors, (e) lack of knowledge, (f) lack of motivation and intention, and (g) low level of self-efficacy and social support (Vancampfort et al., 2013). These findings can help educators and health care service providers to optimize activities involving the lives of young children in many ways. The Mental Health Foundation (n.d.) stated that a clear distinction is often made between mind and body and suggested that the two should not be thought of as separate. This statement corroborates several research evidence that show poor physical health can lead to an increased risk of developing mental health problems. Similarly, poor mental health can negatively impact physical health and lead to an increased risk of some other conditions (see Mental Health Foundation, n.d., p. 1).

MENTAL HEALTH OF YOUNG CHILDREN

Mental disorders among children are described by various organizations in the United States as "serious deviations from expected cognitive, social, and emotional development" (CDC, 2013, p. 1). In the United States, the primary diagnostic tool used to classify mental disorders is the Diagnostic and Statistical Manual of Mental Disorders, 5th ed.; DSM-5 (American Psychiatric Association, 2013). As laid out, the criteria for diagnosing each disorder include the presence of symptoms and certain specific conditions such as functional impairment, age of onset, and symptom duration. The CDC (2013) stated that prevalence of mental disorders, its onset and impact on the child, family, and the community at large, have tremendous impacts on public health in the United States with an estimated total annual cost of $247 billion. A total of 13%–20% of children living in the United States experience some type of mental disorder every year (Morgan et al., 2007; United Nations Children's Fund, 2002), and that surveillance during 1994 to 2011 indicated the prevalence of these conditions are increasing. This trend is particularly worrying to many educators and health care professionals who provide services to children with PMH issues. Kieling et al. (2011) revealed that data on principal diagnosis for hospital stays in the United States from the Healthcare Cost and Utilization Project, reported that, in 2010 mood disorders were among the most common principal diagnosis for all hospital stays among children in the United States; and the rate of hospital stays among children for mood disorders increased 80% during 1997–2010, and from 10 to 17 stay per 10,000 population.

Generally, children with mental disorders may experience serious problems at home when dealing with peer relationships, especially in school. There is evidence that persons with mental disorders frequently have more than one type of disorder, with an estimated 40% of children with one disorder having at least one other mental disorder (CDC, 2013). Other disorders that occur include chronic health conditions (e.g., asthma, diabetes, and epilepsy.) Also, a long-term effect of mental disorder in children is associated with an increased risk for mental disorders in adulthood which can also be associated with decreased productivity, increased substance use and injury, and substantial costs to the individual and society (CDC, 2013). Subsequently, some of these diagnosed mental health disorders in young children present serious challenges and unintended consequences for educators and service providers. For instance, DSM-IV-TR classifies children with ADHD into one of three subtypes corresponding to their symptom profile: predominantly inattentive, predominantly hyperactive and impulsive, or combined (CDC, 2013). It is pertinent to note that the functional limitations related to ADHD symptoms may result in poor academic performance, peer conflicts, and family problems. Also, children with ADHD are more likely to have higher rates of unintentional injuries, emergency department visits, smoking, alcohol use, and illicit substance use (CDC, 2013).

It is important to acknowledge that happy and confident adolescents are most likely to grow into happy and confident adults (Olweus, 1991) who in turn contribute to the health and well-being of nations (Rao, 2001). As Olweus (1991) pointed out, mental well-being among young people especially, have implications for self-esteem, behavior, attendance at school, educational achievement, social cohesion, future health, and life chances (WHO, 2012). Therefore, young children with a good sense of mental well-being possess problem-solving skills, social competence, and a sense of purpose. These assets will help them to rebound from any setbacks that might occur, thrive in the face of poor circumstances, avoid risk-taking behavior, and generally continue a productive life (Morgan & Ziglio, 2007; Scales, 1999). Some risk factors for mental disorders include poverty, social exclusion, violence, peer rejection, isolation, and lack of family support. Certainly, protective factors that help with mental well-being are linked to cohesion at community level, family well-being, individual behaviors and skills, access to adolescent-friendly social services, including health services, and macro-policies (WHO, 2004). Research shows that the more risks young people experience, the worse their developmental outcomes are likely to be and the higher the probability of experiencing psychological distress or mental health disorders. On the contrary, the more opportunities young people have in childhood and adolescence to experience and accumulate positive effects of protective factors that outweigh negative risk factors, the more likely they are to sustain mental health and well-being in later life (Sameroff, Gutman, & Peck, 2003). It is crucial at this time in the United States given the rising number of PMH cases among young children, that certain interventions and strategies be established to help care for the ones diagnosed and prevent common occurrences in the future.

Current data shows that, an estimated 43.6 million adults aged 18 or older had *any mental illness* (AMI) in the United States in 2014. The number of adults who had AMI represents 18.1% of all adults in the United States. In addition, an estimated 9.8 million adults aged 18 or older in the nation had *some mental illness* (SMI) in the past year, and 33.7 million adults had AMI without SMI in the past year. The number of adults with SMI represents 4.1% of all U.S. adults in 2014, and the number of adults with AMI without SMI represents 14.0% of all U.S. adults in 2014. Among adults with AMI in the past year, 22.6% had SMI, and 77.4% did not have SMI (Substance Abuse and Mental Health Services Administration [SAMHSA], 2015). The National Survey on Drug Use and Health (NSDUH) currently does not have an overall measure of mental illness among adolescents aged 12 to 17, but the survey provides estimates of having a past year *major depressive episode* (MDE) and MDE with *severe impairment among adolescents* for this age group (SAMHSA, 2015). What this means is that educators and health care providers must understand that mental health affects how young children think, feel, act, handle stress, relate to others, and make choices. No matter what age, mental health is important at every stage of a person's life. Other factors that may contribute to mental health problems include life experiences such as trauma or history of abuse, biological factors such as genes or chemical imbalances in the brain and family history of mental health problems (SAMHSA, 2013).

TYPES OF MENTAL HEALTH DISORDERS

The WHO explained that although mental health and mental illness are related, they represent different psychological states. Mental health is "a state of well-being in which the individual realizes his or her own abilities, can cope with the normal stresses of life, can work productively and fruitfully, and is able to make a contribution to his or her community" (WHO, 2017a, p. 1). Mental illness on the other hand is defined as "collectively all diagnosable mental disorders" or "health conditions that are characterized by alterations in mental impaired functioning" (U.S. Department of Health and Human Services, 1999, p. 1).

Young children may experience different types of mental health problems that directly or indirectly relate to several of the factors mentioned earlier. Whatever the condition, these are health conditions that either occur for a short period or longer periods with the tendency to affect how the brain functions. For young children, mental health issues can affect their thinking, mood, and behavior in general (SAMHSA, 2013). Below are some critical mental disorders:

- *Anxiety Disorders:* A condition where a person responds to certain objects or situations with fear and dread, may include obsessive compulsive disorders, panic disorders, phobias, and posttraumatic stress disorder (PTSD).
- *Attention Deficit Hyperactivity Disorder (ADHD):* Starts as childhood disorders that can continue through adolescence and adulthood. A child with ADHD may find it difficult to stay focused and pay attention; may have difficulty controlling behavior, and hyperactivity.
- *Eating Disorders:* Involve extreme emotions, attitudes, and behaviors concerning weight and food, such as anorexia, bulimia, and binge eating.
- *Co-occurring Mental and Substance Use Disorder:* A condition where mental illness and substance use disorders occur together. Either one can be a contributing factor or exacerbate the other.
- *Mood Disorders:* Marked by persistent feelings of sadness or periods of feeling overly happy, or fluctuating between extreme sadness and extreme happiness; may include depression, bipolar disorder, seasonal affective disorder (SAD), and compulsion to self-harm.
- *Personality Disorders:* Children who are diagnosed with personality disorders have extreme and inflexible personality traits that are distressing to the person and/or cause problems in work and school or social relationships. They include antisocial personality disorder and borderline personality disorder.

- *Psychotic Disorder:* A person with psychotic disorders hear, see, and believe things that are not real or true, for example, schizophrenia.
- *Substance Use Disorders:* Involve the dependence on or abuse of alcohol and/or drugs, including the nonmedical use of prescription drugs.
- *Suicidal Behavior:* Causes serious problems, immeasurable pain, suffering and loss to individuals, families, and communities. The final result is death.

MENTAL HEALTH CARE AND PROMOTION

The United Nations Children's Fund (2002) recounted the address to the World Conference of Ministers Responsible for Youth in 2002, the former United Nations Secretary General Kofi Annan noted, that a society that cuts itself off from its youth severs its lifeline; it is condemned to bleed to death. In other words, we must not sever our lifeline by paying no attention or failing to provide the needed services for PMH of young children with and without exceptionalities. Mental health indicators show that health care and public health place more emphasis and resources on screening, diagnosis, and treatment of mental illness than mental health per se. These indicators also show that little has been done to maintain the mental health of those free of mental illness (CDC, 2013). Research suggest there are indicators of mental health (Keyes, 1998; Ryff, 1989; Ryff & Keyes, 1995). These indicators represent three domains that may impact a person's life:

- The emotional well-being of the individual such as perceived life satisfaction, happiness, cheerfulness, and peacefulness.
- The psychological well-being of the individual such as self-acceptance, personal growth including openness to new experiences, optimism, hopefulness, purpose in life, control of one's environment, spirituality, self-direction, and positive relationships.
- The social well-being of the individual such as social acceptance, beliefs in the potential of people and society as a whole, personal self-worth and usefulness to society, and sense of community.

Since the aforementioned domains can affect young children's state of PMH, mental health care and promotional activities should be at the top of preventive actions. Activities can consists of interventions to enhance the ability of young children to achieve developmentally appropriate tasks and increase self-esteem, mastery of basic skills, well-being, and social inclusion. All of these will strengthen the ability of young children to cope with adversity. Mental health promotion may depend on several strategies; The WHO (2016b) suggested specific ways to care and promote mental health below:

- early childhood interventions (e.g., home visits for pregnant women, preschool psycho-social activities, and combined nutritional and psycho-social help for disadvantaged populations);
- support to children (e.g., skills building programs and child and youth development programs);
- socioeconomic empowerment of women (e.g., improving access to education and microcredit schemes);
- social support for elderly populations (e.g., befriending initiatives and community and day centers for the aged);
- programs targeting vulnerable groups including minorities, indigenous people, migrants and people affected by conflicts and disasters (e.g., psycho-social interventions after disasters);
- mental health promotional activities in schools (e.g., programs supporting ecological changes in schools and child-friendly schools);
- mental health interventions at work (e.g., stress prevention programs);
- housing policies (e.g., housing improvement);
- violence prevention programs (e.g., reducing availability of alcohol and access to arms);
- community development programs (e.g., integrated rural development);
- poverty reduction and social protection for the poor;
- anti-discrimination laws and campaigns; and
- promotion of the rights, opportunities, and care of individuals with mental disorders.

CONCLUSION

The WHO (2017b) initiated a global school health initiative, to promote the concept of a health-promoting school, a school that is constantly strengthening its capacity as a healthy setting for living, learning, and working. That schools should foster health and learning with all the measures at its disposal. Health and education officials, teachers, students, parents, health care providers, and community leaders should be actively engaged in efforts to make the school a healthy place. It is imperative that the social well-being of the individual, acceptance by peers, and belief in their own potential as a valuable person to the society be established from the young age. Establishing confidence and personal self-worth makes young children think of themselves as being useful to society. In more general terms, society must strive to provide healthy environments, school health education and school health services along with school/community projects and outreach, health promotion programs for staff, opportunities for physical education and recreation, and programs for counseling, social support, and mental health promotion (WHO, 2002). Establishing and implementing good policies and practices that respect an individual's well-being and dignity will certainly provide multiple opportunities for success, as well as personal achievements. Clearly, the school is a significant personal and social environment in the lives of young children; techniques used by general and special educators must be healthy for children, effective with children, protective of children (WHO, 2002), and involved with families, communities, and children.

The value of PMH makes up an integral part of young children's capacity to lead a fulfilling life. It transcends young children's ability to build relationships, learn in school, work or pursue leisure time activities, to include making day-to-day decisions and life choices. Mental health and well-being are influenced not only by individual attributes, but also the social circumstances in which young children may find themselves and the environment in which they live (WHO, 2012). Many factors interact with each other with the potential to threaten or protect an individual's mental health state. For example, risks to mental health manifest themselves at all stages in an individual's life. Notably insecure attachment in infancy or family violence in childhood, can affect mental well-being or predispose one towards mental disorder many years or even decades later (WHO, 2012). Certainly, some people are much more vulnerable to mental disorders in society depending on contexts (e.g., living in poverty, chronic health conditions, being in minority groups, and persons exposed to and/or displaced by war or conflict). To a large measure, young children may be particularly more susceptible to experiencing mental health problems (WHO, 2012). As a result, mental health promotion and protection must be vigorous and broad ranged given the risks inherent in mental health conditions in today's society. Services and interventions need to be multi-layered and multi-faceted so as to establish early recognition and prevent emotional or behavioral problems, especially in childhood and adolescence. Enabling psychosocial development and self-determination (particularly among vulnerable persons) to promote positive interactions within and between social groups would be critical. More importantly, establishing social protection for the poor, anti-discrimination laws and campaigns, and promoting the rights, opportunities, and care of individuals with mental disorders (WHO, 2012) critically necessary for our young children so that they can ensure a stable and promising future in their lives.

REFERENCES

American Psychiatric Association (2013). *Diagnostic and statistical manual of mental disorders, 5th ed.* Retrieved from https://doi.org/10.1176/appi.books.97808 90425596

Asola, E. F., & Obiakor, F. (2016). Inclusion of students with physical disabilities and other health impairments. In J. P. Bakken & F. E. Obiakor (Eds.), *General and special education inclusion in an age of change: Impact on students with disabilities: Advances in special education* (pp. 199–212). Bingley, England: Emerald Group.

Carpenter-Song, E., & Snell-Rood, C. (2017). The changing context of rural America: A call to examine the impact of social change on mental health and mental health care. *Psychiatric Services, 68*(5), 503–506.

Centers for Disease Control and Prevention. (2013). Mental health surveillance among children—United States, 2005–2011. In *MMWR: Morbidity and Mortality Weekly Report,* Supplement, *62*(2), 1–35. Retrieved from https://www.cdc.gov/mmwr/pdf/other/su6202.pdf

Centers for Disease Control and Prevention. (2017). A report of the Surgeon General on physical activity and health adolescents and young adults. Retrieved from https://www.cdc.gov/nccdphp/sgr/adoles.htm

Clay, D. L. (2007). Culturally competent interventions in schools for children with physical health problems. *Psychology in the Schools, 44*(4), 389–396.

Clay, D. L., Mordhorst, M. J., & Lehn, L. (2002). Empirically supported treatments in pediatric psychology: Where is the diversity? *Journal of Pediatric Psychology, 27*(4), 325–337.

Guszkowska, M. (2004). Effects of exercise on anxiety, depression and mood. *Psychiatria Polska, 38*(4), 611–620.

Keyes, C. L. M. (1998). Social well-being. *Social Psychology Quarterly, 61*(2), 121–140.

Kieling, C., Baker-Henningham, H., Belfer, M., Conti, G., Ertem, I., Omigbodun, O., & Rahman, A. (2011). Child and adolescent mental health worldwide: Evidence for action. *Lancet, 378*(9801), 1515–1525. https://doi.org/10.1016/S0140-6736(11)60827-1

Lambert, T. J. R., Velakoulis, D., & Pantelis, C. (2003). Medical comorbidity in schizophrenia. *The Medical Journal of Australia, 178*(Suppl.), S67–S70. Retrieved from https://login.ezproxy.library.valdosta.edu/login?url=http://search.ebscohost.com/login.aspx?direct=true&db=mnh&AN=12720526&site=eds-live&scope=site

Leas, L., & McCabe, M. (2007). Health behaviors among individuals with schizophrenia and depression. *Journal of Health Psychology, 12*(4), 563. Retrieved from https://login.ezproxy.library.valdosta.edu/login?url=http://search.ebscohost.com/login.aspx?direct=true&db=edb&AN=25758637&site=eds-live&scope=site

Mental Health Foundation (n.d.). *Physical health and mental health.* Retrieved from https://www.mentalhealth.org.uk/a-to-z/p/physical-health-and-mental-health#sthash.C2Xu0qSd.dpuf

Morgan, A., Currie, C., Due, P., Gabhain, S. N., Rasmussen, M., Samdal, O., & Smith, R. (2007). M*ental well-being in school-aged children in Europe: Associations with social cohesion and socioeconomic circumstances.* Retrieved from https://pdfs.semanticscholar.org/7716/31b1008f8736fa03c1f19ca55338befa8e43.pdf

Morgan, A., & Ziglio, E. (2007). Revitalising the evidence base for public health: an assets model. *Promotion & Education, Suppl 2,* 17–22.

Olweus, D. (1991). Victimization among school children. *Advances in Psychology, 76,* 45–102. https://doi.org/10.1016/S0166-4115(08)61056-0

Osborn, D., Nazareth, I., & King, M. (2006). Risk for coronary heart disease in people with severe mental illness: Cross-sectional comparative study in primary care. *The British Journal of Psychiatry, 188*(3), 271–277.

Penedo, F. J., & Dahn, J. R. (2005). Exercise and well-being: A review of mental and physical health benefits associated with physical activity. *Current Opinion in Psychiatry, 18,* 189–193. doi:10.1097/00001504-200503000-00013

Rao, M. (2001). Promoting children's emotional well-being: A book review. *Journal of Public Health Medicine, 23*(2), 168–169.

Ryff, C. D., & Keyes, C. L. M. (1995). The structure of psychological well-being revisited. *Journal of Personality and Social Psychology, 69*(4), 719–727.

Ryff, C. D. (1989). Happiness is everything, or is it? Explorations on the meaning of psychological well-being. *Journal of Personality and Social Psychology, 57*(6), 1069–1081.

Sameroff A., Gutman L. M., & Peck S. C. (2003). Adaptation among youth facing multiple risks.   In S. S. Luthar (Ed.), *Resilience and vulnerability: Adaptation in the context of childhood adversities* (pp. 364–391). Cambridge, England: Cambridge University Press.

Scales, P. C. (1999). Reducing risks and building developmental assets: Essential actions for promoting adolescent health. *The Journal of School Health, 69*(3), 113–119.

Shade, B. J., Kelly, C., & Oberg, M. (1997). *Creating culturally responsive classrooms.* Washington, DC: American Psychological Association.

Sofo, S., Nandzo, J., Asola, E. F., & Adjongba, K. S. (2013). African immigrant students' experiences in american physical education classes. *International Journal of Arts and Commerce, 2*(10), 59–70.

Substance Abuse and Mental Health Services Administration. (2013). Community conversations about mental health: Information briefs. Rockville, MD: Author. Retrieved from https://store.samhsa.gov/system/files/sma13-4763.pdf

Substance Abuse and Mental Health Services Administration. (2015). Behavioral health trends in the United States: Results from the 2014 National Survey on Drug Use and Health. Retrieved from https://www.samhsa.gov/data/sites/default/files/NSDUH-FRR1-2014/NSDUH-FRR1-2014.pdf

United Nations Children's Fund. (2002). *Adolescence: A time that matters.* New York, NY: Division of Communication. Retrieved from https://www.unicef.org/pub_adolescence_en(1).pdf

United States Census Bureau. (2003). *Statistical abstract of the United States.* Washington, DC: Author. Retrieved from https://www.census.gov/library/publications/2003/compendia/statab/123ed.html

U.S. Department of Health and Human Services. (1999). *Mental health: A report of the Surgeon General.* Rockville, MD: Author. Retrieved from https://profiles.nlm.nih.gov/ps/access/NNBBHS.pdf

Vancampfort, D., Correll, C. U., Probst, M., Sienaert, P., Wyckaert, S., De Herdt, A.,. . . , De Herta, M. (2013) A review of physical activity correlates in patients

with bipolar. *Journal of Affective Disorders, 145*(3), 285–291. https://doi.org/10
.1016/j.jad.2012.07.020

World Health Organization. (2002). *Skills for health. Skills-based health education including life skills: An important component of a child-friendly/health-promoting school.* Geneva, Switzerland: Author. Retrieved from http://www.who.int/
school_youth_health/media/en/sch_skills4health_03.pdf

World Health Organization. (2004). *Prevention of mental disorders: Effective interventions and policy options: Summary report.* Geneva, Switzerland: Author. Retrieved from http://www.who.int/mental_health/evidence/en/prevention_of_mental_
disorders_sr.pdf

World Health Organization. (2012). *Risks to mental health: An overview of vulnerabilities and risk factors.* Geneva, Switzerland: Author. Retrieved from http://www.
who.int/mental_health/mhgap/risks_to_mental_health_EN_27_08_12.pdf

World Health Organization. (2014). *Mental health: A state of well-being.* Geneva,
Switzerland: Author. Retrieved from http://www.who.int/features/factfiles/
mental_health/en/

World Health Organization. (2016a). *Constitution of the World Health Organization.*
Geneva, Switzerland: Author. Retrieved from http://apps.who.int/gb/bd/
PDF/bd47/EN/constitution-en.pdf?ua=1

World Health Organization. (2016b). *Mental health: Strengthening our response.* (Fact
sheet). Geneva, Switzerland: Author. Retrieved from http://www.who.int/
mediacentre/factsheets/fs220/en/

World Health Organization (2017a). *South-East Asia Journal of Public Health, 6*(1),
1–98. Geneva, Switzerland: Author. Retrieved from http://www.searo.who.
int/publications/journals/seajph/issues/seajphv6n1.pdf

World Health Organization (2017b). *School and youth health: Global school health initiative.* Geneva, Switzerland: Author. Retrieved from https://www.who.int/
school_youth_health/gshi/en/

CHAPTER 9

USING TECHNOLOGY TO EDUCATE YOUNG CHILDREN WITH AND WITHOUT DISABILITIES

Emily C. Bouck, Emma Sipila, Sarah B. Avendano, and Jeffrey P. Bakken

Technology is increasingly used in schools and homes, and young children are not immune from the influx of technology in one's daily life (Herold, 2016; Plowman, 2015). Although technology use has increased for all, including young children, individuals debate the merits of technology use in the home and the school. The controversy regarding technology use is probably most centered on young children, particularly when considering technology involving screens (e.g., computers, tablets, smartphones, and televisions; American Academy of Pediatrics, 2010; Plowman, McPake, & Stephen, 2012). Screen time for young children is associated with negative implications such as the increased likelihood of obesity, lower academic achievement, decreased language development, and poorer quality or quantity of adult interactions (Barr, Lauricella, Zack, & Calvert, 2010; Duch,

Educating Young Children With and Without Exceptionalities, pages 119–134
Copyright © 2019 by Information Age Publishing

Fisher, Ensari, & Harrington, 2013; Mendelsohn et al., 2008; Schmidt et al., 2012; Tomopoulos et al., 2010). Although, other researchers have found no negative associations or some determined positive associations that exist with regard to academic content for young children as a result of interaction with sophisticated technology (e.g., computers; Clements & Sarama, 2007; Penuel et al., 2009; Plowman & McPake, 2013; Primavera, Wiederlight, & DiGiacomo, 2001). In fact, it is argued the "what" of young children and technology (i.e., the content) is more important than the "how" (i.e., via screen; National Association for the Education of Young Children and the Fred Rogers Center, 2012).

Regardless of the debate, technology use for young children is not likely to end. As noted, young children are exposed to technology in the home and in their educational settings. This chapter discusses the use of technology for children with and without disabilities. For young children with disabilities, the conversation moves beyond everyday technologies that children may interact with in their homes or educational settings, and includes a discussion of a special type of technology for individuals with disabilities—assistive technology.

TECHNOLOGY FOR YOUNG CHILDREN

Young children today are surrounded by a wide array of technologies used in multiple ways throughout their day (Bers, 2008; Cooper, 2005; Parette, Quesenberry, & Blum, 2010). Over time, the use of technology in classrooms has increased and it plays a more prevalent role in early childhood education today than previously. The amount of computer usage in early childhood classrooms has increased dramatically over time. Why has this happened? The potential benefits of computers in early childhood settings are supported by research (Clements, 1994; Fletcher-Flinn & Suddendorf, 1996; Haugland, 1996; Lomangino, Nicholson, & Sulzby, 1999). For example, Clements (1994) reported that computers can enhance social interaction, motivation, and attitudes toward learning. Computers also help to increase collaboration and improves cognitive benefits (Clements, 1994; Lomangino et al., 1999). The appropriate use of computers can facilitate young children's development of academic abilities such as oral language, reading, and writing skills (Clements, 1994). The most powerful benefits of computers are that they foster children's higher level thinking and mathematical abilities such as sorting, counting, and numerical recognition (Corning & Halapin, 1989).

Assistive technology has been known to increase survival skills of young children with disabilities. The power of assistive technology to enable young children with disabilities to participate in family, school, and community activities is becoming widely recognized (Judge, 2006). Thus, professionals are responsible for helping children and families select and acquire assistive technology devices and equipment as well as instructing them in their use (Judge, 2006). Agencies that serve young children, however, are struggling to meet the challenges of technology use in a manner that provides appropriate technology, the training of professionals and families in the use of assistive technology, and demonstrating unique ways for families to access assistive technology in a timely and reasonable manner (Judge & Parette, 1998; Lesar, 1998; Mistrett, Lane, & Ruffino, 2005). Young children need immediate access to appropriate devices as they grow. However, the current system for acquiring assistive technology often requires a lengthy process of referral and assessment (Judge, 2006) and getting the actual technology for the children is delayed. Although the use of assistive technology for young children is increasing, the lack of awareness and the lack of training continue to act as major barriers to providers using assistive technology (Judge & Parette, 1998; Lesar, 1998).

It is important to note that the National Association for Education of Young Children (NAEYC; 1996), the leading association and accreditation organization in the early childhood field, strongly suggested that technology should be integrated into early childhood practice physically, functionally, and philosophically. The organization recommended that technology should be integrated into the daily routine of classroom activities.

Mobile Technology

As technology has evolved, a new type of computer, the mobile device (e.g., smartphone and tablet), has gained popularity. The mobile device is a small-sized, portable computer that typically has touch screen features; the iPad is one of the more popular mobile devices used in schools today (Ok, Kim, Kang, & Bryant, 2016). Although the use of mobile devices is sometimes seen as negative, teachers and parents reported positive results using mobile devices and apps, and professionals also demonstrated that mobile devices and apps have the potential to be useful tools for students with disabilities (Korner & Leske, 2012). Mobile devices provide the availability of downloadable, inexpensive software that can serve as cost-effective assistive technology (Douglas, Wojcik, & Thompson, 2011). In addition, their touch screen features allow students with disabilities to use the device without having to operate a mouse or a touch pad. Most mobile devices also have Internet access, built-in video, a camera, and audio-capture capabilities (Korner & Leske, 2012). These devices can be easily individualized to meet the needs of individual students with disabilities.

Educational Apps

With the addition of mobile technology, many apps have been created, with a multitude focusing on educational aspects. Many parents of struggling students and teachers who work with them seek apps that are valid for academic improvement (Ok et al., 2016).

By the Fall of 2013, there were approximately one million apps available online (Costello, 2018) and more apps are being released daily (Buckler & Peterson, 2012). Apps can be used in a variety of technological devices. For example, mobile device apps are designed for use on smartphones (e.g., iPhone, Google Pixel), tablet computers (e.g., iPads), and e-readers (e.g., Kindle Fire, Nook), whereas online apps are designed for personal computers that are connected to the Internet (More & Travers, 2013). An analysis of the iTunes App Store found that 60% of the most frequently downloaded educational apps targeted toddlers and preschool-age children as the primary user, and only 16% targeted elementary, middle, or high school students (Shuler, 2009).

According to the Division for Early Childhood of the Council for Exceptional Children (DEC), technology applications have the potential to help young children with disabilities more easily participate in the general education curriculum as well as obtain access to the natural environment (Stremmel, 2005). DEC stated that the use of technology in early childhood education settings may improve children's quality of life (Stremmel, 2005). Not only can technology be used to improve instruction and access, but it may also provide a way to assess children's understanding and development (Mulligan, 2003). Some early childhood professionals might assume that apps in the education category of a marketplace are developmentally appropriate. The reality is that many of these apps may be lacking essential design, instruction, content, accessibility, and individualization features that are characteristics of high-quality educational software (More & Travers, 2013). Thus, early childhood professionals must thoughtfully evaluate educational apps and use existing guidelines for appropriate practice before integrating them into their classroom (see More & Travers, 2013).

Early childhood professionals must examine apps to determine whether they align with developmentally appropriate practices (DAPs). DAP is an approach that affirms the child is an active participant in the learning process (Copple & Bredekamp, 2009). When DAP is implemented in an early childhood setting, the child constructs meaning and knowledge by interacting with material as well as people. DEC suggested that DAP requires professionals to consider not only the child's developmental age but also his or her chronological age (Wolery, 2005). The content of the app should be related to the child's individualized education program (IEP)/individual family service plan (IFSP) goals and outcomes, and be challenging enough for the child to make progress in the general curriculum while also ensuring the content is not so difficult that it elicits frustration (see More & Travers, 2012). In addition, educational apps should avoid rote memorization and should not be a version of an electronic worksheet (Haugland, 2005).

Software

The other challenging issue is software selection. A number of researchers recommend that when used with appropriate software and teaching strategies, the computer is a tool that can enhance children's learning (Wright, 1998). Choosing software from the huge quantity of programs is overwhelming for most teachers. Haugland (1997) suggested that developmental software that reflects the needs and interests of children is open ended and easy to use, and updated is preferable for early childhood teachers.

TECHNOLOGY FOR YOUNG CHILDREN WITH DISABILITIES

Technology for young children with disabilities encompasses the technology options for students without disabilities. Technology for young children also involves a special type of technology—assistive technology. Assistive technology devices, by definition, are "any item, piece of equipment, or product system, whether acquired commercially, modified, or customized, that is used to increase, maintain, or improve functional capabilities of individuals with disabilities (29 U.S.C. Sec 2202[2])"; Technology-Related Assistance for Individuals With Disabilities Act, 1990). In other words, assistive technology devices are tools designed to help an individual with a disability.

Assistive Technology

As stated, assistive technology devices are tools individuals with disabilities use to increase their independence, improve their quality of life, provide for participation, and offer access to materials and environments (Blackhurst, 2005; Bouck, 2017). Assistive technology devices represent a broad range of tools and technologies, ranging from no-tech (e.g., mnemonics and sign language) to low-tech options (e.g., a pencil grip and a grabber) to medium-tech options (e.g., battery operated moving toys and books on tape) to high-tech options (e.g., apps and tablets and motorized wheelchairs; Bouck, 2017). Assistive technology devices are also used for a wide range of purposes, including adaptive environments, adaptive toys and games, augmentative and alternative communication, computer access, instructional aids, mobility, and positioning (Bryant & Bryant, 2003, 2012).

As indicated, assistive technology devices are important for many individuals with disabilities, including young children with disabilities. For young children with disabilities, assistive technology devices provide greater access to participation as well as independence in their daily lives. Assistive technology devices for young children with disabilities run the gamut and embrace the federal definition of anything, as assistive technology for young children includes not just commercial for-purchase tools, but also those made or modified by parents or educators (Bouck, 2017; Mistrett, Lane, & Ruffino, 2005). While assistive technology devices for young children include the full range of assistive technology categorization, for young children, areas of primary emphases include movement, communication, interactions with one's environment, and emerging academics (Bouck, 2017; Lane & Mistrett, 2002). In this chapter, in addition to focusing on these four main areas of assistive technology devices for young children, we also highlight emerging assistive technologies for young children.

Movement

Movement refers to an individual's ability to move within an environment or between environments (Carver, Ganus, Ivey, Plummer, & Eubank, 2015). Assistive technology devices can be used with individuals with disabilities who may need assistance moving throughout their environment, including young children (Carver et al., 2015; Mistrett, Lane, & Goetz, 2000). Exploration and interaction with the environment via movement are crucial for child development; and assistive technology devices can provide opportunities to children with physical disabilities or others who need assistance to move independently (Wiart, 2011). When thinking of assistive technology devices for movement, one typically envisions a wheelchair. Yet, movement-based assistive technology devices are much more, including walkers, canes, gait trainers, and automatic door openers (Bouck, 2017). Like all types of assistive technology, assistive technology devices for movement can range from low-tech to high-tech (see Table 9.1).

Low-tech assistive technology options (e.g., walkers, gait trainers, canes, crutches, and manual wheelchairs) are generally available, inexpensive, and easy to use. Walkers, designed for children to stand behind and push as they walk, can be commercially purchased; parents and educators of young children who would benefit from a walker can also repurpose young children's moving toys, such as a shopping cart or activity centers on wheels (Lane & Mistrett, 2002). However, parents and educators should be cautious that commercially-available toys—as opposed to specifically designed and marketed walkers—provide the necessary stability and weight needed if the individual does not have the necessary posture control (Lowry &

TABLE 9.1 Examples of Assistive Technology Devices for Young Children With Disabilities

	No-Tech	Low-Tech	Medium-Tech	High-Tech
Movement		Gait trainers	Automatic door openers	Power wheelchairs
Communication	Sign language	Picture exchange communication system (PECS)	Attainment talkers	Proloquo2Go app for iPad
Interactions with environment		Suction-based dishes	Switch-compatible battery-operated toy	Environmental control units
Academics	Fingers for counting in mathematics	Large print books	Audio books	Ebooks

Hatton, 2002). Gait trainers are similar to walkers, as they are wheeled de-vices, but they provide additional support if the individual cannot put full weight on their legs or have a weak trunk control, strength, balance, or range of motion (Paleg & Livingstone, 2015).

While perhaps not commonly known as assistive technology, an auto-matic door opener can serve to increase the functional capabilities of a young child with a disability. Automatic door openers—typically found in buildings by their entrance and exit doors—allow an individual to press a button to open the door, instead of manually opening the door. This en-ables a young child to easily and independently gain access into the build-ing, classroom, or public location.

The most commonly associated assistive technology device to support movement for young children is a wheelchair. There are two main types of wheelchairs: manual and power (i.e., electric or motorized; Srinivasan & Lloyd, 2011). A manual wheelchair is a chair with wheels that is operated by the individual gripping his/her hands on the wheels and pushing the wheels forward. This type of wheelchair is considered low-tech and may be less expensive than a powered wheelchair. However, if an individual has poor hand strength or muscle weakness, it could make using manual wheelchairs more challenging, especially for young children with disabili-ties (Bouck, 2017). Power wheelchairs can be operated using any body part through the use of various controls such as a joystick (Karp, 2008; Srini-vasan & Lloyd, 2011). Although some debate exists regarding when to in-troduce a power wheelchair as opposed to a manual wheelchair for young children with disabilities, researchers found young children can success-fully use such devices (Guerette, Furumasu, & Tefft, 2013; Jones, McEwen, & Neas, 2012).

Communication

Technology is basically used for communication. As Gargiulo (2015) pointed out, communication is "the exchange of ideas, information, thoughts, and feelings" (p. 365); technology is most typically referred to as augmentative and alternative communication (AAC; Bouck, 2017). AAC is broad and refers to tools or devices, aside from oral speech, that allow individuals to express themselves. AAC technologies include those that either enhance (i.e., augment) a young child's communication or serve as the principal mode of communication (i.e., alternative; Hanline, Nunes, & Worthy, 2007). AAC devices, like all other categories of assistive technology, include no-tech, low-tech, medium-tech, and high-tech options (refer to Table 9.1). AAC devices are also categorized as unaided and aided. Unaided AAC refers to a communication system that is on a person's body; that is, nothing is external to the user. A typical example of an unaided AAC is sign language (American Speech-Language-Hearing Association [ASHA], n.d.; Beukelman & Mirenda, 2013; Bouck, 2017). Communication systems that utilize something external to the person (i.e., a device or tool) are referred to as aided; these include app-based AAC tools, picture-based systems, and battery-operated devices (Beukelman & Mirenda, 2013; Bouck, 2017).

Although perspectives can vary, some researchers suggest implementing AAC with even young children, such as those under one year of age (Reichle, Beukelman, & Light, 2002). While historically, there may have been a general tendency to wait to implement AAC with young children with complex communication needs, researchers do suggest that AAC use is beneficial for speech production and does not negatively impact speech development in children (Millar, Light, & Schlosser, 2006; Reichle, Drager, Caron, & Parker-McGowan, 2016; Schlosser & Wendt, 2009).

Interactions With the Environment

Assistive technology devices that promote or support young children's interaction with their environments also focus around play or daily living (Bouck, 2017). Many of the assistive technology tools to support young children's interactions with the environment are more low-tech or medium-tech; these items can also be commercially purchased, made, modified, or repurposed (i.e., using an item for a purpose other than its original intention; Mishra & Koehler, 2009). One type of assistive technology that can support young children's interactions with their environments are switches (Baker, 2014; Bouck, 2017). Switches are assistive technology devices that allow young children to interact with a variety of other technologies, tools, or devices, including battery-operated toys, computers, wheelchairs, and light switches (Assistive Technology Training Online Project, 2000–2005; York & Fabrikant, 2011). For young children the most common application may be battery-operated toys (Baker, 2014). A variety of different types of switches exist; switches can range from ones in which one presses to activate, to those that respond via proximity or puffing (Cook & Polgar, 2015; York & Fabrikant, 2011). The range of switches is expansive so that if a young child is able to move or activate any part of his/her body—including breathing or raising an eyebrow—a switch exists for him or her to use.

While switches provide a commercially made, for-purchase assistive technology option to support young children's interactions with the environment, many everyday items can also be repurposed to be assistive technology to support kids in their environments and with play (Bouck, 2017). Repurposed or for-purchase assistive technology devices within a young child's environments can support such actions as stabilizing, attaching, extending, highlighting, and confining (Mistrett et al., 2005). In terms of stabilizing, educators and parents can use grip shelf liner to stabilize play and everyday objects for young children. Educators and parents can also purchase specially designed dishes, such as plates or bowls with suctions, to aid in stabilizing while eating. For attaching, toys and everyday items can be applied with Velcro to aid young children get an item. A squishy ball or popsicle sticks can be used to extend items, such as books for turning pages or crayons for easier grasp. Of course, for-purchase items like puzzles with wooden knobs or enlarged or triangular crayons can also aid in extending. Wikki sticks or simply colored yarn can be highlight items for young children. Finally, inflatable pools, cookies sheets, and hula-hoops can confine toys for young children, keeping items within their vicinity and reach (Baker, 2014; Bouck, 2017; Mistrett et al., 2005; Sadeo & Robinson, 2010).

Academics

For K–12 students, devices and tools to support academics is one of the major purposes of assistive technology. For young children with disabilities, assistive technology devices can also support academics and/or emerging academics (Hsin, Li, & Tsai, 2014). Assistive technology devices for academics run the gamut, from low-tech options (e.g., large print books, concrete manipulatives) to more high-tech options (e.g., apps, e-books, and virtual manipulatives; refer to Table 9.1). Although literature is limited and still emerging regarding assistive technology devices to support young children with disabilities in academically oriented domains, researchers suggested young children's—including those with and without disabilities—learning was positively impacted from exposure to technology with regards to academic domains (Hsin et al., 2014). Specifically, Hsin, Li, and Tsai (2014) found six areas of focus for technology and young children in which the results were positive, as opposed to resulting in a negative effect: (a) language and literacy, (b) mathematics, (c) science, (d) cognitive abilities, (e) digital literacies, and (f) other.

One of the areas in which assistive technology devices are increasingly used to support young children with disabilities is in literacy. Literacy-based assistive technology devices have become progressively more common among young children and are accessible means to encourage literacy development for young children with disabilities (Miller & Warschauer, 2014; Scholastic, 2015). A range of options exists to support literacy via assistive technology devices. For one, parents can use an older technology of audio books in which the book is read via CD (or even online now with speech-to-text computer or mobile device capabilities) and young children can follow along with a physical book or on the screen (Bouck, 2017). Such audio books can be easily found in libraries and bookstores. Alternatively, options exist for parents to purchase a specifically designed book and the parent (or any other adult or older child) can record themselves reading a book so a child can follow along in the printed book while listening to the recording of the text (Bouck, 2017). Some companies even produce specifically marketed e-books or interactive digital academic literacy tools (i.e., masked as toys) for young children (Bouck, 2017). For example, LeapFrog™ offers several products that encourage interactive reading such as specialized pens for use with specific books that can read text at the word, sentence, or page level.

Another interactive literacy program for young children targeted for educator use is Headsprout (Lazel, 2017). Headsprout teaches a range of literacy skills from reading fundamentals for non-readers to comprehension for Grades 3–5, and adapts the instruction to individual learner performance (see https://www.headsprout.com/). This allows for instruction to be presented at a pace suitable for the young child so that a skill is mastered before moving on to more complex skills. Headsprout can be independently operated by students; however, the computerized instruction can also be mediated by a parent or educator to support the use of the technology by the student (Plavnick et al., 2016).

Emerging Technologies

A final element of assistive technology for young children reviewed is emerging technologies. Although research and practical use of emerging technologies is limited, the emerging technologies of today may be the technologies or assistive technologies of tomorrow for young children with disabilities. Examples of today's emerging technologies for young children with disabilities include wearables (e.g., FitBit®), augmented reality (e.g., Pokemon Go), and virtual reality (Adams Becker et al., 2016). Other emerging technologies better harnessing the power of mobile technologies, such as tablets (e.g., iPad) and smartphones, for young children and the use of robots (Kim & Smith, 2015).

One increasingly popular technology for young children with and without disabilities are apps (Bouck, 2017). A multitude of apps exist for young children. When using apps for young children with disabilities, educators and parents must be careful in their consideration and selection. More and Travers (2013) suggested apps for use with young children with disabilities be evaluated with regards to their accessibility, their use of "developmentally appropriate practices" (i.e., actively engage the child as well as are age appropriate), their content (i.e., free from violence and stereotypes), and their relevance to a child's goals or need per his or her IEP or IFSP).

CONCLUSION

For better or worse, technology is ever-present in our society and that is unlikely to change. Young children are not immune from the increasing presence of technology in their daily lives and educational settings. And although some concern and resistance occur with technology and young children (e.g., Barr et al., 2010; Duch et al., 2013; Mendelsohn et al., 2008; Schmidt et al., 2012; Tomopoulos et al., 2010), technology offers support and opportunities for young children, especially young children with disabilities. These children benefit from a specialized form of technology—assistive technology, which serves to increase their independence, interactions, and functional capabilities. As with technology for any child, technology—including assistive technology—considerations and implementation for young children must be deliberate and value-added. In other words, technology for the sake of technology does not benefit young children with or without disabilities, but technology that extends what the child is doing or learning, makes opportunities possible, and improves quality of life or learning benefits (Webster, 2017).

REFERENCES

Adams Becker, S., Freeman, A., Giesinger Hall, C., Cummins, M., & Yuhnke, B. (2016). *NMC/CoSN horizon report: 2016 k–12 edition.* Austin, Texas: The New Media Consortium. Retrieved from http://cdn.nmc.org/media/2016-nmc-cosn-horizon-report-k12-EN.pdf

American Academy of Pediatrics. (2010). Media education. *Pediatrics, 126*(5), 1012–1017. doi:10.1542/peds.2010-1636.

American Speech-Language-Hearing Association. (n.d.). *Communication services and supports for individuals with severe disabilities: FAQs: Basic information about augmentative and alternative communication.* Retrieved from http://www.asha.org/NJC/faqs-aac-basics.html

Assistive Technology Training Online Project. (2000–2005). *Switch users.* Retrieved from http://atto.buffalo.edu/registered/ATBasics/Populations/Switch/print module.php

Baker, F. S. (2014). Engaging in play through assistive technology: Closing gaps in research and practice for infants and toddlers with disabilities. In. B. DaCosta & S. Seok (Eds.), *Assistive technology research, practice, and theory* (pp. 207–221). Hershey, PA: IGI Global.

Barr, R., Lauricella, A., Zack, E., & Calvert, S. L. (2010). Infant and early childhood exposure to adult-directed and child-directed television programming: Relations with cognitive skills at age four. *Merrill-Palmer Quarterly, 56*(1), 21–48. Retrieved from http://www.ericdigests.org/2003-1/assistive.htm

Bers, M. U. (2008). *Blocks to robots: Learning with technology in the early childhood classroom.* New York, NY: Teachers College Press.

Beukelman, D. R., & Mirenda, P. (2013). *Augmentative and alternative communication: Management of severe communication disorders in children and adults* (4th ed.). Baltimore, MD: Brooks.

Blackhurst, A. (2005). Perspectives on applications of technology in the field of learning disabilities. *Learning Disability Quarterly, 28*(2), 175–178.

Bouck, E. C. (2017). *Assistive technology.* Thousand Oaks, CA: SAGE.

Bryant, D., & Bryant, B. (2003). *Assistive technology for people with disabilities.* Boston, MA: Allyn & Bacon.

Bryant, D., & Bryant, B. (2012). *Assistive technology for people with disabilities* (2nd ed.). Boston, MA: Allyn & Bacon.

Buckler, T., & Peterson, M. (2012). Is there app for that? Developing an evaluation rubric for apps for use with adults with special needs. *Journal of BSN Honors Research, 5*(1), 38–56. Retrieved from archie.kumc.edu/handle/2271/1092

Carver, J., Ganus, A., Ivey, J. M., Plummer, T., & Eubank, A. (2015). The impact of mobility assistive technology devices on participation for individuals with disabilities. *Disability and Rehabilitation: Assistive Technology, 11*(6), 468–477.

Clements, D. H. (1994). The uniqueness of the computer as a learning tool: Insights from research and practice. In J. L. Wright & D. D. Shade (Eds.), *Young children: Active learners in a technological age* (pp. 31–50). Washington, DC: NAEYC.

Clements, D. H., & Sarama J. (2007). Effects of a preschool mathematics curriculum: Summative research on the *Building Blocks* project. *Journal for Research in Mathematics Education, 38*(2), 136–63.

Cook, A. M., & Polgar, J. M. (2015). *Assistive technologies: Principles and practice* (4th ed.). St. Louis, MO: Elsevier.

Cooper, L. Z. (2005). Developmentally appropriate digital environments for young children. *Library Trends, 54*(2), 286–302.

Copple, C., & Bredekamp, S. (2009). *Developmentally appropriate practice in early childhood programs serving children from birth through age 8* (3rd ed.). Washington, DC: National Association for the Education of Young Children.

Corning, N., & Halapin, J. (1989, March). *Computer applications in the action-oriented kindergarten.* Paper presented at the meeting of the Connecticut Institute for Teaching and Learning Confernece. Wallinfor, CT

Costello, S. (2018). How many apps are in the iPhone app store. *Lifewire.* Retrieved from https://www.lifewire.com/how-many-apps-in-app-store-2000252

Douglas, K. H., Wojcik, B. W., & Thompson, J. R. (2011). Is there an app for that? *Journal of Special Education Technology, 27*(2), 59–70.

Duch, H., Fisher, E. M., Ensari, I., & Harrington, A. (2013). Screen time use in children under 3 years of old: A systematic review of correlates. *International Journal of Behavioral Nutrition and Physical Activity, 10,* 102–111.

Fletcher-Flinn, C. M., & Suddendorf, T. (1996). Do computers affect the mind? *Journal of Educational Computing Research, 15*(2), 97–112.

Gargiulo, R. (2015). *Special education: Contemporary society* (5 ed.). Thousand Oaks, CA: SAGE.

Guerette, P., Furumasu, J., & Tefft, D. (2013). The positive effects of early powered mobility on children's psychosocial and play skills. *Assistive Technology, 25*(1), 39–48. doi:10.1080/10400435.2012.685834

Hanline, M. F., Nunes, D., & Worthy, M. B. (2007). Augmentative and alternative communication in the early childhood years. *Beyond the Journal: Young Children on the Web. 62*(4), 1–6.

Haugland, S. (1996). Enhancing children's sense of self and community through utilizing computers. *Early Childhood Education Journal, 23*(4), 227–230.

Haugland, S. (1997). Children's home computer use. *Early Childhood Education Journal, 25*(2), 133–135.

Haugland, S. W. (2005). Selecting or upgrading software and web sites in the classroom. *Early Childhood Education Journal, 32*(5), 329–340.

Herold, B. (2016, February 5). Issues A–Z: Technology in education: An overview. *Education Week.* Retrieved September 18, 2017 from http://www.edweek.org/ew/issues/technology-in-education/

Hsin, C., Li, M., & Tsai, C. (2014). The influence of young children's use of technology on their learning: A review. *Journal of Educational Technology & Society, 17*(4), 85–99.

Jones, M. A., McEwen, I. R., & Neas, B. R. (2012). Effects of power wheelchairs on the development and function of young children with severe motor impairments. *Pediatric Physical Therapy, 24*(2), 131–140. doi:10.1097/PEP.0b013e31824c5fdc

Judge, S. L. (2006). Constructing an assistive technology toolkit for young children: Views from the field. *Journal of Special Education Technology, 21*(4), 17–24.

Judge, S. L., & Parette, H. P. (Eds.). (1998). *Assistive technology for young children with disabilities: A guide to providing family-centered services.* Cambridge, MA: Brookline Books.

Karp, G. (2008). *Life on wheels: The a to z guide to living fully with mobility issues.* New York, NY: Demos Medical.

Kim, Y., & Smith, D. (2015). Pedagogical and technological augmentation of mobile learning for young children interactive learning environments. *Interactive Learning Environments, 25*(1), 4–16. doi:10.1080/10494820.2015.1087411

Korner, H., & Leske, G. (2012). Apps for communication and everyday living. *Independent Living, 28*(1), 21–24.

Lane, S. J., & Mistrett, S. (2002). Let's play! Assistive technology intervention for play. *Young Exceptional Children, 5*(2), 19–27.

Lazel Inc. (2017). Learning A–Z. *Headsprout.* Retrieved, September 10, 2017 from https://www.headsprout.com/

Lesar, S. (1998). Use of assistive technology with young children with disabilities: Current status and training needs. *Journal of Early Intervention, 21*(2), 146–159.

Lomangino, A. G., Nicholson, J., & Sulzby, E. (1999). The influence of power relations and social goals on children's collaborative interactions while composing on the computer. *Early Childhood Research Quarterly, 14*(2), 197–228.

Lowry, S. S., & Hatton, D. D. (2002). Facilitating walking by young children with visual impairments. *RE: view, 34*(3), 125–133.

Mendelsohn, A. L., Berkule, S. B., Tomopoulos, S., Tamis-LeMonda, C. S., Huberman, H. S., Alvir, J., & Dreyer, B. P. (2008). Infant television and video exposure associated with limited parent–child verbal interactions in low socioeconomic status households. *Archives of Pediatrics & Adolescent Medicine, 162*(5), 411–417.

Millar, D. C., Light, J. C., & Schlosser, R. W. (2006). The impact of augmentative and alternative communication intervention on the speech production of individuals with developmental disabilities: A research review. *Journal of Speech, Language, and Hearing Research, 49*(2), 248–264.

Miller, E. B., & Warschauer, M. (2014). Young children and e-reading: Research to date and questions for the future. *Learning, Media, and Technology, 39*(3), 283–305. doi:10.1080/17439884.2013.867868

Mishra, P., & Koehler, M. (2009). Tool cool for school? No way! Using the TPACK framework you can have your hot tools and teach with them, too. *Learning & Leading With Technology, 36*(7), 14–18.

Mistrett, S., Lane, S., & Goetz, A. (2000). *A professional's guide to assisting families in creating play environments for children with disabilities. Let's Play! Project 1995–2000.* Buffalo, NY: University at Buffalo: Center for Assistive Technology.

Mistrett, S. M., Lane, S. L., & Ruffino, A. (2005). Growing and learning through technology: Birth to five. In D. Edyburn, K. Higgins, & R. Boone (Eds.), *The handbook of special education technology research and practice* (pp. 273–307). Whitefish Bay, WI: Knowledge by Design.

More, C. M., & Travers, J. C. (2013) What's app with that? Selecting educational apps for young children with disabilities. *Young Exceptional Children, 16*(2), 15–32.

Mulligan, S. A. (2003). Assistive technology: Supporting the participation of children with disabilities. *Young Children, 58*(6), 50–51.

National Association for the Education of Young Children. (1996). NAEYC position statement; Technology and young children—ages three through eight. *Young Children, 51*(6), 11–16.

National Association for the Education of Young Children and the Fred Rogers Center. (2012). *Technology and interactive media as tools in early childhood programs serving children from birth through age 8.* Retrieved from http://www.naeyc.org/files/naeyc/file/positions/PS_technology_WEB2.pdf

Ok, M. W., Kim, M. K., Kang, Y. K., & Bryant, B. R. (2016). How to find good apps: An evaluation rubric for instructional apps for teaching students with learning disabilities. *Intervention in School and Clinic, 51*(4), 244–252.

Paleg, G., & Livingstone, R. (2015). Outcomes of gait trainer use in home and school settings for children with motor impairments: A systematic review. *Clinical Rehabilitation, 29*(11), 1077–1091.

Parette, H. P., Quesenberry, A. C., & Blum, C. (2010). Missing the boat with technology usage in early childhood settings: A 21st century view of developmentally appropriate practice. *Early Childhood Education Journal, 37*(5), 335–343.

Penuel, W. R., Pasnik, S., Bates, L., Townsend, E., Gallagher, L. P., Llorente, C., & Hupert, N. (2009). *Preschool teachers can use a media-rich curriculum to prepare low-income children for school success: Results of a randomized controlled trial.* New York, NY: Education Development Center.

Plavnick, J. B., Thompson, J. L., Englert, C. S., Mariage, T., & Johnson, K. (2016). Mediating access to headsprout® early reading for children with autism spectrum disorders. *Journal of Behavioral Education, 25*(3), 357–378. doi:10.1007/s10864-015-9244-x

Plowman, L. (2015). Researching young children's everyday uses of technology in the family home. *Interacting with Computers, 27*(1), 36–46. doi:10.193/iwc/iwu031

Plowman, L., & McPake, J. (2013). Seven myths about young children and technology. *Childhood Education, 89*(1), 27–33. doi:10.1080/00094056.2013.757490

Plowman, L., McPake, J., & Stephen, C. (2012). Extending opportunities for learning: The role of digital media in early childhood education. In S. Suggate & E. Reese (Eds.), *Contemporary debates in childhood education and development* (pp. 95–105). New York, NY: Routledge.

Primavera, J., Wiederlight, P. P., & DiGiacomo, T. M. (2001, April). *Technology access for low-income preschoolers: Bridging the digital divide.* Paper presented at the American Psychological Association Annual Meeting, San Francisco, CA. Retrieved from www.knowledgeadventure.com/jumpstartworld/_docs/ChildTechnology_White_Paper.pdf

Reichle, J., Beukelman, D., & Light, J. (2002). *Exemplary practices for beginning communicators: Implications for AAC.* Baltimore, MD: Brookes.

Reichle, J., Drager, K., Caron, J., & Parker-McGowan, Q. (2016). Playing the long game: Considering the future of augmentative and alternative communication research and service. *Seminars in Speech and Language, 37*(4), 259–273. doi:10.1055/s-0036-1587706

Sadeo, K. C., & Robinson, N. B. (2010). *Assistive technology for young children: Creating inclusive learning environment.* Baltimore, MD: Paul H. Brookes.

Schlosser, R. W., & Wendt, O. (2009). Effects of augmentative and alternative communication intervention on speech production in children with autism: A systematic review. *American Journal of Speech-Language Pathology, 17*(3), 212–230.

Schmidt, M. E., Haines, J., O'Brien, A., McDonald, J., Price, S., Sherry, B., & Taveras, E. M. (2012). Systematic review of effective strategies for reducing screen time among young children. *Obesity, 20*(7), 1338–1354. doi:10.1038/oby.2011.348

Scholastic. (2015). Kids & family reading report (5th ed.). Retrieved from http://www.scholastic.com/readingreport/Scholastic-KidsAndFamilyReadingReport-5thEdition.pdf

Shuler, C. (2009). *iLearn: A content analysis of the iTunes app store's education section.* Retrieved from http://www.joanganzcooneycenter.org/Reports-21.html

Srinivasan, S., & Lloyd, L. L. (2011). Assistive technology for mobility, seating, and positioning. In O. Wendt, R. W. Quist, & L. L. Lloyd (Eds.), *Assistive technology: Principles and applications for communication disorders and special education* (pp. 413–446). Bingley, England: Emerald.

Stremmel, K. (2005). DEC recommended practices: Technology applications. In S. Sandall, M. L. Hemmeter, B. J. Smith, & M. E. McLean (Eds.), *DEC recommended practices: A comprehensive guide for practical application in early intervention/early childhood special education* (pp. 147–162). Missoula, MT: DEC.

Technology-Related Assistance for Individuals With Disabilities Act, 29 U.S.C. § 2201 *et seq.*

Tomopoulos, S., Dreyer, B. P., Berkule, S., Fierman, A. H., Brockmeyer, C., & Mendelsohn, A. L. (2010). Infant media exposure and toddler development. *Archives of Pediatrics & Adolescent Medicine, 164*(12), 1105–1111.

Webster, M. D. (2017). Philosophy of technology assumptions in educational technology leadership. *Educational Technology & Society, 20*(1), 25–36.

Wiart, L. (2011). Exploring mobility options for children with physical disabilities: A focus on powered mobility. *Physical & Occupational Therapy in Pediatrics, 31*(1), 16–18. doi:10.3109/01942638.2011.532452

Wolery, M. (2005). DEC recommended practices: Child focused practices. In S. Sandall, M. L. Hemmeter, B. J. Smith, & M. E. McLean (Eds.), *DEC recommended practices: A comprehensive guide for practical application in early intervention/early childhood special education* (pp. 71–76). Missoula, MT: DEC.

Wright, J. L. (1998). A new look at integrating technology into the curriculum. *Early Childhood Education Journal, 26*(2), 107–109.

York, C. S., & Fabrikant, K. B. (2011). High technology. In O. Wendt, R. W. Quist, & L. L. Lloyd (Eds.), *Assistive technology: Principles and applications for communication disorders and special education* (pp. 221–264). Bingley, England: Emerald.

CHAPTER 10

THE ROLE OF EDUCATOR PREPARATION PROGRAMS IN THE EDUCATION OF YOUNG CHILDREN

**Ying Hui-Michael, Kalli Kemp,
and Beth Pinheiro**

The changing landscape of the American workforce throughout the years, particularly the increase of mothers working outside of the home, has had impacts on education for young children (Laughlin, 2013; U.S. Department of Health and Human Services and U.S. Department of Education, 2016). With more parents working, demands for high quality early childhood care and education for children from birth to 5 years old is increasing. Laughlin (2013) recounted the Census Bureau that noted that approximately 61% of children under Age 5 spent regular time in some type of childcare. On average, these children spent approximately 33 hours per week in childcare. Enrollment in state-funded preschool has also risen over the years, with approximately 1.5 million children attending a state-funded program (Barnett et al., 2017). Parents want assurances that their young children are not only

Educating Young Children With and Without Exceptionalities, pages 135–152
Copyright © 2019 by Information Age Publishing
135

being taken care of in a safe and nurturing environment, but they also want their children to attend high quality childcare and education programs that promote their children's development and learning (U.S. Department of Health and Human Services, n.d.). This has led to an increased focus on the status of early childhood care and education programs.

National and local initiatives and policies have given increasing attention to supporting and promoting the learning and development of all children before they enter school. This interest can be seen in various federal and state initiatives designed to improve program quality for young children. Many states have developed early childhood policies and initiatives that are meant to promote healthy development and school readiness, so young children have a better chance of later success in school and beyond. In the last decade, a number of significant grants were endowed to focus on improving early learning and development programs. The 2015 Every Student Succeed Act (ESSA) gave $250 million annually for a new, redesigned preschool development grant program. Other federal initiatives such as the Child Care and Development Block Grant (CCDBG) Act, and Race to the Top's Early Learning Challenge (RTT-ELC) grant competition also provided financial incentives for high quality early childhood care and education programs. The interest in investing in early childhood care and education programs continues to grow. This is not only because of the growing demand for out-of-home childcare, but also because of the recognition of the critical importance of educational experiences during the early years.

High quality early childhood care and education programs have positive impacts on child development outcomes. Studies have found that attending high quality early childhood educational settings leads to both short- and long-term gains in a number of areas such as cognitive development, social-emotional development (Barnett, 2008; Burchinal et al., 2008; Peisner-Feinberg et al., 2001), language development (Burchinal et al., 2008; Peisner-Feinberg et al., 2001), math ability, and behavioral development (Peisner-Feinberg et al., 2001). While research suggests that all children benefit, children from socio-economically disadvantaged backgrounds seem to benefit the most from high quality early childhood education (Barnett, 2008). Reynolds, Ou, and Temple's (2018) longitudinal study of a large-scale program revealed that the school-based preventive intervention for children in poverty was associated with educational attainment in midlife. The researchers found that these intervention programs resulted in higher rates of high school graduation, college attendance, and degree completion. It should also be noted that high quality early childhood education has shown to have economic benefits, including increasing parental employment (Barnett, 2008).

With interest in improving the quality of early childhood education programs, it is important to consider the role of institutions of higher education

(IHEs) in this process. The primary responsibility IHEs have regarding program quality is in preparing the early childhood teacher workforce. Various studies have indicated (e.g., Hyson, Horn, & Winton, 2012; Maxwell, Lim, & Early, 2006; Washington, 2008) that IHEs fail to meet the growing needs in the field of early childhood care and education. Many schools, colleges and departments of education have called for and invested in reinventing early childhood education preparation programs to meet the early childhood care and education community needs. With the need for high quality early childhood care and education in mind, we outline the demand for highly effective educators of young children. We also discuss current practices and challenges in early childhood education teacher preparation programs and outline recommendations for IHEs to improve the capacity and quality of teacher education for early childhood care and education professionals.

A CALL FOR EFFECTIVE TEACHERS OF YOUNG CHILDREN

The demand for high quality teachers of young children stems from two sources. First, teachers of young children need to work adequately with a diverse generation of children who spend time in a wide range of settings from birth through Age 5. Second, the field has an escalating demand for early childhood care and education professionals to have formal training in early care and education.

RESPONDING TO DIVERSE NEEDS

Education of children from Kindergarten to Grade 12 is fairly consistent across the country, with services primarily provided by public schools. The system regulating services for children from birth to 5 years old is much more diverse (Institute of Medicine & National Research Council, 2015; Whitebook, Gomby, Bellm, Sakai, & Kipnis, 2009). Children may be cared for and educated in a variety of programs including federally and state funded early childhood programs such as Early Head Start, Head Start, state funded prekindergarten, early intervention, and early childhood special education programs. Many children may also receive care and education in home-based programs and private center-based programs. Furthermore, the system is complicated by various agencies that oversee early childhood education. There is not a specific agency, such as the department of education, that oversees services provided to children under the age of five (Whitebook et al., 2009). Finally, early childhood education encompasses a wide range of ages in which children have a wide range of needs. Services provided to infants and toddlers may be distinctly different than those provided to preschoolers preparing for entry into school.

The ever-changing American demographics also entail improvement of preparedness of early childhood professionals. As the American population is growing more diverse, more children come from nontraditional American families. Today, 1 in 5 American children are in poverty. African American, Native American, and Hispanic children are disproportionately low income and "poor" socioeconomically (Children's Defense Fund, 2016). The number and portion of young children from culturally and linguistically diverse (CLD) backgrounds are increasing. It is estimated that almost 50% of children under five in the United States are non-White (U.S. Census Bureau, 2012). Many federally and state funded early childhood care and education programs also reflect high percentage of young English learners (ELs). For example, almost one-third of children in Head Start are ELs (National Clearinghouse for English Language Acquisition and Language Instruction Education Programs, 2011). Furthermore, increasing numbers of young children who have disabilities and are at high risk are in early childhood care and education programs. The Division for Early Childhood (DEC) of the Council for Exceptional Children and National Association for the Education of Young Children (NAEYC) have called for early childhood inclusion practices. In their joint position statement, the two organizations stated that quality childhood care and education programs must demonstrate inclusive practices that provide best care and education to all children (DEC/NAEYC, 2009). Given the diversity in the field, teachers of young children must understand children's developmental changes and support children's learning and development within the sociocultural context of the family, education setting, community, and broader society.

FORMAL TRAINING IN EARLY CHILDHOOD EDUCATION

The fields of early childhood care and education have historically relied on informal apprenticeship. Expectation that a teacher must have a bachelor's degree and be certified in the subjects taught in PreK–12 public education is more consistent and in place compared to teachers of young children. According to the National Survey of Early Care and Education Project Team (2013), approximately 53% of center-based early childhood teachers have an associate's degree or higher. Educational attainment tends to be higher for teachers of older children, such as teachers in preschool and kindergarten settings compared to infants and toddlers in early childhood care settings. The State of Preschool 2016 report (Barnett et al., 2017) noted that 35 state funded preschool programs across the country require a bachelor's degree for teachers, and 51 programs require teachers have specialized training in PreK. Early and Winton (2001) found that teachers with a bachelor's degree are more likely to work in elementary school settings while those with associate's degrees are more likely to work with younger children in community-based settings.

One significant discussion around high quality teachers of young children has been arguments on teachers' levels of education. Arguments favoring higher levels of education have indicated there are relationships between teachers' education levels and classroom quality. In reviewing multiple studies, Barnett (2003) indicated that teachers with higher levels of education are more likely to have a number of positive characteristics such as sensitive and responsive interactions that benefit children in their classrooms. Pianta et al. (2005) found that teachers with a bachelor's degree fostered a more positive emotional climate in their classrooms than other teachers, and training or education in early childhood had some impact on classroom quality. Burchinal, Cryer, Clifford, and Howes (2002) found that teachers with a bachelor's degree in infant-toddler and preschool classrooms were rated higher on assessments of classroom quality than teachers who did not have a bachelor's degree. Vu, Jean, and Howes (2008) also found that teachers with a bachelor's degree plus a master permit performed better on assessments of classroom quality.

On the other hand, not all research has shown a consistent or strong link between program quality and teacher education. Early et al. (2006) found only slightly higher scores on measures of classroom quality for teachers with a bachelor's degree compared to teachers without a bachelor's degrees. Furthermore, only math skills of children were higher when their teachers had more education. Other child outcomes were not significantly different based on teacher education. In another study, Early et al. (2007) examined seven studies that had researched the connection between teacher qualifications and classroom quality/child outcomes. The researchers were unable to find a clear connection between teacher educational attainment and classroom quality. While these results seem troubling, the researchers suggest that these results do not necessarily mean that teachers do not need high levels of education.

While there have been debates about whether a college degree is a necessary qualifying element, public recognition on the formal education and expertise necessary to be an effective teacher of young children is growing. In fact, early childhood education advocates (e.g., Pianta et al., 2005) have expressed the need for all early childhood teachers to have at least a bachelor's degree, and majoring in early childhood education or state certification to provide service to young children. No Child Left Behind federal legislation and Good Start Grow Smart, its early childhood education companion, have also stressed the importance of highly-qualified professionals to children's later success, and having an appropriate college degree is an indicator of highly-qualified teachers. The field seems to be uniting on the idea that PreK teachers should have a bachelor's degree and that all teachers should be encouraged to increase their education to that level.

CURRENT STAGE OF EARLY CHILDHOOD TEACHER PREPARATION PROGRAMS

Trends in preparing high quality teachers have focused on the requirement of a bachelor's degree or better in the subject taught; and they have also focused on being certified and being able to demonstrate knowledge in the subject taught. Unfortunately, early childhood teacher preparation programs experience the lack of program and personnel capacities to meet growing community needs as they are understaffed and under resourced at all levels (Washington, 2008). In reviewing the existing literature and communicating with colleagues, we identify the following issues in early childhood education programs: (a) a lack of program capacity and faculty and student diversity for degree programs, and (b) inadequacies in preparing early childhood education professionals for three groups of children (i.e., birth to 3-year-old children, young children with disabilities, and young children from CLD backgrounds). It must be noted that most empirical studies in early childhood education teacher preparation were conducted in the first decade of the century; this phenomenon indicates the lack of recent data in early childhood education preparation research.

Program and Personnel Capacities

The national report on early childhood teacher programs in the United States (Maxwell, Lim, & Early, 2006) noted among all IHEs that offer associate's, bachelor's, master's or doctoral degrees in any discipline, only 30% of two- and four-year IHEs have some type of early childhood preparation programs available. Maxwell et al. (2006) also found that not all early childhood programs are administratively housed with education departments or schools. They are also offered in a variety of departments including social or behavioral sciences, child development or family studies, health related and human services. Therefore, these program curricula may vary.

It appears early childhood education is low in status with many teacher education programs. Early childhood education programs often have a low number of full time faculty and lower qualifications of faculty. For instance, Whitebook, Bellm, Lee, and Sakai (2005) found that about two-thirds of faculty members at California's early childhood teacher preparation programs are part-time faculty. Compared to other programs of their institutions, there are fewer full-time early childhood faculty members and they serve more students than do faculty in other programs. Both national and state level data also reflects that many early childhood faculty members may also lack both training and direct work experience with young children. According to Maxwell et al.'s (2006) national survey, among all IHEs that offer early childhood education, only 54% of early childhood faculty had a degree in early care and education or a related field, and about 75% had experience working with young children. About 27% of faculty hold doctoral degrees, with about 53% at four-year colleges and 8% at two-year colleges.

Other challenges related to low numbers of full-time faculty members are advising and supporting teacher candidates. As the field continues to advocate for increasing education of the early childhood workforce, IHEs will experience increasing enrollment of nontraditional early childhood education teacher candidates who present unique needs in academic support. While they enjoy learning and are highly motivated, they also encounter a variety of barriers in college. They may lack academic confidence and preparation for college work, have a difficult time balancing work life, school life, and personal life, and may experience financial strain. Research suggests that without strong support, many nontraditional teacher candidates are more likely to quit school without completing a degree (Whitebook et al., 2005). Also, Maxwell et al.'s (2006) national level survey on early childhood teacher preparation programs found that most faculty members in early childhood teacher preparation programs were White. On the other hand, teacher candidates in early childhood teacher preparation programs seem more diverse than typical faculty. The study found that about 20% of full time faculty members were non-White, compared to 37% CLD teacher candidates in all early childhood education degree programs, 46% in associate's degree programs, 31% in bachelor's programs, 34% in master's programs, and 36% in doctoral programs, respectively. While it is encouraging to see teacher candidates in early childhood teacher preparation programs are more diverse than faculty, it is also important to note that CLD teacher candidates are less represented in bachelor's, master's, and doctoral degrees than in associate's degree programs.

Preparation for All Children

The knowledge and skills of teachers are among the most important elements in shaping how much a young child learns (Early et al., 2007). Lobman, Ryan, and McLaughlin (2005) emphasized that early childhood teacher preparation program curriculum should include four key areas: foundations of early education, pedagogy of teaching content areas such as literacy and math, knowledge and skills in teacher–child interactions, and field-based experiences with young children. Although many early childhood programs prepare teachers to work with children from birth to 8 years old, they may not adequately prepare teacher candidates to work with students in each particular age group. The tendency has been that teacher education programs do not provide adequate training on children's development and education in the early years, especially the birth to 3-year-old period (Early & Winton, 2001). According to Early and Winton (2001), approximately 79% of bachelor's programs devoted at least an entire course to the education of preschool children while only approximately 40% devoted at least an entire course to the education of infants and toddlers. Associate's programs more frequently devoted at least an entire course to infant and toddler education with approximately 60% of programs offering such courses. Recent graduates from programs that prepared candidates in early childhood education and early childhood special education birth–kindergarten reported that they were better prepared to work with young children ages 3 years old to kindergarten than birth to 3 years old (Miller & Losardo, 2002). Teachers who take a position in an early childhood care setting may not be prepared to support young children's learning and development because the teacher preparation curriculum they were taught focuses on older children.

Considering that many teachers in the early childhood field will work in inclusive environments that serve both students with typical development and students with disabilities, coursework on working with young students with disabilities should be included in early childhood programs. Teacher preparation programs nationwide include some training on students with disabilities, usually in the form of one course over the entire program. Chang, Early, and Winton (2005) found that the majority of both bachelor's and associate's programs do require a course in working with young students with disabilities. However, only bachelor's programs were more likely to require field-based experiences related to this content. This content is important for early childhood teachers, as studies have shown that teachers have more favorable views of inclusion when they have received training on disabilities (Mulvihill, Shearer, & Van Horn, 2002). Miller and Losardo (2002) surveyed recent graduates of blended early childhood education and early childhood special education programs covering birth to kindergarten. The recent graduates noted that their programs provided opportunities and prepared them to work with students with mild disabilities. However, they noted that they had fewer opportunities to work with students with moderate to severe disabilities, and their programs would benefit from additional instructions and opportunities in this area. They do not feel fully prepared to work with all young students with varying disabilities.

It is important to note that IHEs also need to provide better teacher training on issues of social, linguistic, and cultural diversity. Maxwell et al. (2006) evaluated coursework and practical experiences provided in 1,179 two- to four-year institutions across the United States. They found that about 20% of associate's programs and about 10% of bachelor's and master's programs did not require any coursework in working with bilingual children learning English as a second language. Early childhood education faculty observe that early childhood education program teacher candidates (a) may not acknowledge how social and cultural factors influence a child and parent's behavior, (b) lack the understanding of ELs' language development, (c) do not know how to support a child's home language, and (d) have biases towards racial/ethnic minority children and families (Whitebook et al., 2009). Whitebook et al. (2009) also found that although IHE program faculty recognize the inadequate preparation for teacher candidates in urban poverty, and CLD learners, teacher preparation programs still struggle to find best approaches to address these students' needs effectively.

PREPARING HIGHLY QUALIFIED PROFESSIONALS OF YOUNG CHILDREN

IHEs are clearly obligated to improve and sustain the quality of early childhood education preparation to prepare highly qualified early childhood professionals who are (a) knowledgeable in subjects and young children and families, (b) skilled to provide service and instruction, and (c) able to demonstrate good professional dispositions. Educator preparation programs in all pathways (e.g., undergraduate, graduate, and certification programs) must address these important factors to adequately prepare early childhood teachers to respond to the needs in the field. The needs of young children and families are complex and involve multiple factors (e.g., CLD backgrounds, medical needs, poverty, and young and single mothers). Early childhood education programs must respond to complex needs to prepare teachers who are competent to serve all children and collaborate with other professionals. In the following sections, we present essential competencies that highly qualified early childhood educators should master.

Essential Knowledge, Skills, and Professional Dispositions

Teacher preparation programs should focus on early childhood educators' competencies of what a highly qualified early childhood teacher knows and does, and provide course work and clinical experiences that align with standards reflecting such competencies (Early et al., 2007). The National Association for Education of Young Children (NAEYC, 2009) established standards for early childhood educator competencies. NAEYC's professional standards describe the following competencies: (a) promoting child development and learning, (b) building family and community relationships, (c) evaluation to support young children and families, (d) applying effective approaches to interact with children and families, (e) designing and implementing meaningful instruction, and (f) demonstrating professionalism as an early childhood educator. In addition, NAEYC's (2009) position statement emphasized the importance of teacher preparation programs covering a broad age span, from infant/toddlers to early elementary school. Early childhood educators should master a broad knowledge of development and learning across the birth through Age 8 range. They should also be acquainted with broad knowledge and skills of assessment and instruction across the age span. Furthermore, NAEYC (2009) suggested that early childhood educators should master in-depth knowledge and skills in at least two of three periods: infants/toddlers, preschool/prekindergarten, and early grades.

In addition to content related competencies, professional dispositions are imperative. NAEYC (2009) defined that effective early childhood teachers display five professional behaviors: (a) having a strong identification and involvement with the field; (b) understanding the ethical standards professional guidelines; (c) collaborating with other professionals and families to inform practice; (d) demonstrating commitment to knowledgeable, reflective, and critical approaches; and (e) engaging informed advocacy for young children and families and their practice. Early childhood teachers in the field also identify characteristics they believe are integral to effective teaching. Colker (2008) surveyed 43 early childhood educators who pinpointed 12 characteristics; namely, (a) passion about children and teaching, (b) perseverance, (c) risk taking, (d) pragmatism, (e) patience, (f) flexibility, (g) respect, (h) creativity, (i) authenticity, (j) love of learning, (k) high energy, and (l) sense of humor. Early childhood teacher preparation programs can use these professional indicators as guiding principles to develop teacher candidates' professional dispositions and characteristics.

Cultural Competency

Preparing culturally and linguistically responsive early childhood educators is one of the essential goals for teacher preparation programs. The NAEYC's (2009) recommendations on responding to linguistic and cultural diversity state that early childhood educators must respect and nurture diversity, and prompt both English language acquisition and fostering children's home languages and cultural identities. Research from social scientists and teacher educators has suggested the principles of multicultural education for better understanding the significance of culture, class, and language to foster knowledge, skills, and dispositions that will result in more culturally responsive and competent educators and other professionals (Ladson-Billings,1995; Sleeter, 2007). These and other researchers and practitioners offer the theoretical, conceptual, and pedagogical conventions that emphasize the importance of preparing teachers and helping professionals to develop (a) knowledge bases about cultural diversity and perspectives in practices, (b) abilities to respond to cultural and linguistic diversity in instruction and services, and (c) caring and committed professional qualities to build diverse communities.

Villegas and Lucas (2002) explained that teacher preparation programs should prepare teacher candidates to not view the world through their own narrow cultural, class, and linguistic lenses. They need to be aware of their own views, the views of their students, and examine and reflect on the relevance of these views in teaching and learning. Teacher preparation programs must prepare teacher candidates to develop foundational, historical, and contemporary social knowledge base of their students. Although it may not be realistic to expect pre-service teachers to gain distinct and accurate knowledge of all cultural groups in any given school, they should and can gain an initial understanding of the facts of different cultural groups and their views of education. Clearly, culturally and linguistically responsive early childhood educators (a) appreciate cultural heritages of their own and of young children and families; (b) recognize that cultural and linguistic experiences that young children bring to their programs are essential to their cognitive, language and emotional development; and (c) look at cultural and linguistic implications to everyday learning and teaching in working with young children and families.

Ability to Work With Young Children with Disabilities

Increasing diversity has exposed the large number of children with disabilities and other special learning needs who attend early childhood programs. Early childhood educators often provide direct service to young children who have developmental delays and disabilities and their families. In 2014, DEC of the Council for Exceptional Children proposed inclusive practices in the following areas: leadership, assessment, environment, family, instruction, interaction, teaming, and collaboration. DEC (2014) recognized that the best early childhood educators cannot implement best practice in a vacuum. Leadership in early childhood intervention and education is important. Recommendations of those who provide leadership reflect the quality to (a) lead for an early childhood organization; (b) collaborate with families, professionals and varying communities; and (c) develop, refine and implement policies and procedures to improve the outcomes of young children with exceptional needs. Early childhood educators need to demonstrate knowledge and skills in the following areas: (a) assessment for disability diagnoses, program and instructional decisions; (b) provision of positive physical, social and sequential environments to support children with disabilities to access maximum learning opportunities; (c) provision of family-centered programming, strengthening parent capacity practices, and building relationships with families; (d) designing and implementing early intervention and early childhood special education instruction to maximize learning and improve outcomes of children with disabilities; (e) using sensitive and responsive interactional practices to foster all children's learning; (f) collaborating with family members and colleagues from multiple disciplines to ensure appropriate and effective services to young children with disabilities and families; and (g) assisting in various transitions (e.g., from early intervention to community or school based programs) for children with disabilities.

Content in special education should prepare early childhood teacher candidates to work with students with a variety of disabilities including those considered moderate or severe. It is important that educators feel prepared to provide instruction to all students in the classrooms they serve. Additionally, appropriate instruction with birth to 3-years-old age group is particularly important in early childhood special education programs that prepare teacher candidates to work in early intervention (EI). Strategies and service delivery may vary substantially for this age group. Bruder and Dunst (2005) identified several areas of service delivery in EI in which IHEs should prepare teacher candidates. These areas include (a) family-centered practices, (b) cross-disciplinary models and collaboration, (c) service coordination, (d) individualized family service plan (IFSP) development, and (e) service delivery in natural environments. Services in EI are provided in young children's natural environments, which often include the child's home; and teacher candidates must be prepared to work with families and their children in these environments.

RECOMMENDATIONS FOR EDUCATOR PREPARATION PROGRAMS

Facing the need to prepare well-educated early childhood teachers requires IHEs to increase program capacity to offer early care and education workforce to obtain college degrees. Reinventions of early childhood teacher preparation have occurred in many states, and IHEs are being asked to collaborate with others to respond to the need for teacher preparation for all children. The reinvented early childhood teacher preparation includes promising initiatives that emphasize easy training access, partnership with different organizations, national accreditations, and inclusive models (Washington, 2008).

Connecting to Accreditation

Due to the variation in types of early childhood education programs offered through different pathways, it is imperative that early childhood education preparation programs meet professional standards for early childhood teachers. An early childhood education program can improve greater quality assurance on what an early childhood educator knows and does by meeting national specialized professional association and state licensure requirements. At the national level, NAEYC higher education accreditation awards accreditations to early childhood teacher education programs. The accreditation process provides a framework for program evaluation, self-study, and improvement in the quality of early childhood teacher preparation programs. Not only do the accreditation processes improve program quality, earning accreditation can also increase awareness among college administrators of the early childhood program and its value to college community, and in turn, help colleges to create additional partnerships with community stakeholders (NAEYC, n.d).

Blending Diversity and Exceptionality

Adapting program models to prepare teachers to work with all young children, including those who are CLD, and those with disabilities will prepare teacher candidates for the realities. Early childhood programs can blend diversity and exceptionality to allow program candidates to take coursework in early childhood education, special education, and English as a second language. Through an integrated program study, teacher candidates may also have opportunities to be certified in early childhood education, special education and/or teaching English as a second language. Such program design provides a model of how integrated coursework from the three fields can prepare early childhood teacher candidates to respond to current challenges in serving young children and families from CLD backgrounds and those with disabilities.

Diversifying Field Experiences

Field experiences are integral parts of teacher preparation programs. They are designed to give teacher candidates guided experiences with early childhood professional mentors in the field. It is essential that teacher preparation programs offer diverse educational settings (e.g., rural, urban, public, and private settings) that cover the span of birth through 8 years old. Diversifying field experiences is more needed than ever while the U.S. populations are becoming increasingly diverse. Culp, Chepyator-Thomson, and Hsu (2009) found that teacher candidates who participate in diverse field experiences have a higher appreciation for the diversity of their students. Early childhood researchers and practitioners (e.g., Culp et al., 2009; Daniel & Friedman, 2005) have suggested that teacher preparation programs provide service learning or practicum experiences associated with coursework and also provide opportunities to work with diverse children and families in a wide range of settings.

Supporting Non-Traditional Teacher Candidates

As many nontraditional teacher candidates arrive in teacher preparation programs, IHEs must provide the practice that focuses on educational support and financial assistance. We recommend (a) offering classes online and alternative delivery modules (e.g., weekend classes, site-based model); (b) providing academic support (e.g., tutoring); (c) using student cohorts and learning communities for bilingual teacher candidates to increase language and emotional support; (d) increasing advising and counseling to help teacher candidates familiarize themselves with academic structure; and (e) providing financial incentives (e.g., using state and federal grants to support tuition). Program candidates who come from CLD backgrounds may face language barriers in academic work. The bilingual early childhood model offers classes and materials in English and the candidates' native language, provides enriched program training, and prepares future early childhood bilingual teachers for the diverse field.

Diversifying the Faculty

As early childhood education program teacher candidates become increasingly diverse, the effort to have a diverse faculty body becomes ever more imperative. Individual IHEs and professional organizations have published numerous handbooks, guides, and strategies for recruiting and retaining diverse faculty. Besides supporting these existing efforts, IHEs must pipeline diverse teacher candidates to graduate education. It is difficult to reinvent higher education without preparing new instructors and leaders. Master's and doctoral programs need to recruit diverse early childhood teachers who have appropriate early care and education expertise.

Increasing Training for Leadership

Many professionals with a bachelor's or master's degree will become program administrators and supervisors. Educator preparation programs need to provide opportunities for these leaders to increase competency in early childhood education. Leaders at the early childhood level need to not only have knowledge of child development and learning, they must also hire and support staff in implementing instructional strategies that benefit young children. Early childhood programs, particularly those at the master's level, should provide course work that emphasizes leadership. These courses should consider the unique contexts that exist for early childhood education and should include content that covers both administration and management of organizations and early childhood development and instruction.

CONCLUSION

As the demand for high quality early childhood care and education for children from birth to five years old continues to increase, IHEs will continue to face the need to increase capacity to prepare effective professionals to teach young children. Education preparation programs for early childhood education must acknowledge that the field's urgent need is to have formally trained early childhood professionals who can meet the diverse and complex needs of today's young children and families. Education preparation programs need to continue to develop and improve programs to prepare future early childhood educators who are competent in the content knowledge, skills, and disposition in working with all children and families. These programs need to consistently evaluate their practices and reinvent programs and curriculum designs. Their vision must go beyond simply responding to the needs in the field, but also to making efforts to lead the education of young children.

REFERENCES

Barnett, W. S. (2003). *Better teachers, better preschools: Student achievement linked with teacher qualifications. Preschool Policy Matters (2).* New Brunswick, NJ: National Institute for Early Education Research.

Barnett, W. S. (2008). *Preschool education and its lasting effects: Research and policy implications* (EPRU Policy Brief). Boulder and Tempe: Education and the Public Interest Center & Education and Policy Research Unit. Retrieved July 24, 2017 from https://nepc.colorado.edu/sites/default/files/PB-Barnett-EARLY-ED _FINAL.pdf

Barnett, W. S., Friedman-Krauss, A. H., Weisenfeld, G. G., Horowitz, M., Kasmin, R., & Squires, J. H. (2017). *The state of preschool 2016. National Institute for Early Education Research.* Retrieved July 24, 2017 from http://nieer.org/ state-preschool-yearbooks

Burchinal, M. R., Cryer, D., Clifford, R. M., & Howes, C. (2002). Caregiver training and classroom quality in child care centers. *Applied Developmental Science, 6*(1), 2–11.

Burchinal, M., Howes, C., Pianta, R., Bryant, D., Early, D., Clifford, R., & Barbarin, O. (2008). Predicting child outcomes at the end of kindergarten from the quality of pre-kindergarten teacher–child interactions and instruction. *Applied Development Science, 12*(3), 140–153.

Bruder, M. B., & Dunst, C. J. (2005). Personnel preparation in recommended early intervention practices: Degree of emphasis across disciplines. *Topics in Early Childhood Special Education, 25*(1), 25–33.

Chang, F., Early, D. M., & Winton, P. J. (2005). Early childhood teacher preparation in special education at 2- and 4-year institutions of higher education. *Journal of Early Intervention, 27*(2), 110–124.

Children's Defense Fund. (2016). *Children poverty in America 2015: National analysis.* Washington, DC: Author.

Colker, L. J. (2008). Twelve characteristics of effective early childhood teachers. *Journal of the National Association for the Education of Young Children, 63*(3), 96–106.

Culp, B. O, Chepyator-Thomson, J. R, & Hsu, S.-H. (2009). Pre-service teachers' experiential perspectives based on a multicultural learning; service practicum. *Physical Educator, 66*(1), 23–26.

Daniel, J., & Friedman, S. (2005). Taking the next step, preparing teachers to work with culturally and linguistically diverse children. *Beyond the Journal, Young Children on the Web.* National Association of Young Children. Retrieved from http://www.buildinitiative.org/WhatsNew/ViewArticle/tabid/96/ArticleId/ 258/Taking-the-Next-Step-Preparing-Teachers-to-Work-with-Culturally-and -Linguistically-Diverse-Young-Chi.aspx

Division for Early Childhood. (2014). *DEC recommended practices in early intervention/ early childhood special education. 2014.* Retrieved from http://www.dec-sped .org/dec-recommendedpractices

Division for Early Childhood and the National Association for the Education of Young Children. (2009). *Early childhood inclusion: A joint position statement of the Division for Early Childhood (DEC) and the National Association for the Education of Young Children (NAEYC).* Chapel Hill, NC: The University of North Carolina, FPG Child Development Institute.

Early, D. M., Bryant, D. M., Pianta, R. C., Clifford, R. M., Burchinal, M. R., Ritchie, S.,... & Barbarin, O. (2006). Are teachers' education, major, and credentials related to classroom quality and children's academic gains in pre-kindergarten? *Early Childhood Research Quarterly, 21*(2), 174–195.

Early, D. M., Maxwell, K. L., Burchinal, M., Alva, S., Bender, R. H., Bryant, D.,...& Henry, G. T. (2007). Teachers' education, classroom quality, and young children's academic skills: Results from seven studies of preschool programs. *Child Development, 78*(2), 558–580.

Early, D. M., & Winton, P. J. (2001). Preparing the workforce: Early childhood teacher preparation at 2- and 4-year institutions of higher education. *Early Childhood Research Quarterly, 16*(3), 285–306.

Hyson, M., Horn, D. M., & Winton, P. J. (2012). Higher education for early childhood educators and outcomes for young children: Pathways toward greater effectiveness. In R. Pianta (Ed.), *Handbook of early childhood education* (pp. 553–583). New York, NY: The Guilford Press.

Institute of Medicine and National Research Council. (2015). *Transforming the workforce for children birth through age 8: A unifying foundation.* Retrieved from https://www.nap.edu/resource/19401/BirthtoEight_brief.pdf

Ladson-Billings, G. (1995). Toward a theory of culturally relevant pedagogy. *American Educational Research Journal, 32*(3), 465–491.

Laughlin, L. (2013). *Who's minding the kids? Child care arrangements. Current Population Reports,* P70–135. Washington, DC: U.S. Census Bureau.

Lobman, C., Ryan, S., & McLaughlin, J. (2005). Reconstructing teacher education to prepare qualified preschool teachers: Lessons from New Jersey. *Early Childhood Research and Practice, 7*(2), 515–540.

Maxwell, K. L., Lim, C.-I., & Early, D. M. (2006). *Early childhood teacher preparation programs in the United States: National Report.* Chapel Hill, NC: The University of North Carolina, FPG Child Development Institute.

Miller, P. S., & Losardo, A. (2002). Graduates' perceptions of strengths and needs in interdisciplinary teacher preparation for early childhood education: A state study. *Teacher Education and Special Education, 25*(3), 309–319.

Mulvihill, B. A., Shearer, D., & Van Horn, M. L. (2002). Training, experience, and child care providers' perceptions of inclusion. *Early Childhood Research Quarterly, 17*(2), 197–215.

National Association for the Education of Young Children. (n.d). *Benefits of NAEYC higher education accreditation.* Retrieved from https://www.naeyc.org/accreditation/higher-ed/accreditation-benefits

National Association for the Education of Young Children. (2009). *NAEYC standards for early childhood professional preparation programs, A position statement of the National Association for the Education of Young Children.* Retrieved from https://www.naeyc.org/sites/default/files/globally-shared/downloads/PDFs/resources/position-statements/2009%20Professional%20Prep%20stds Revised%204_12.pdf

National Clearinghouse for English Language Acquisition and Language Instruction Education Programs. (2011). *Key demographic & practice recommendations for young English learners.* Retrieved July 17, 2017 from https://files.eric.ed.gov/fulltext/ED564265.pdf

National Survey of Early Care and Education Project Team. (2013). *Number and characteristics of early care and education (ECE) teachers and caregivers: Initial findings from the National Survey of Early Care and Education (NSECE), OPRE Report #2013-38,* Washington, DC: Office of Planning, Research and Evaluation,

Administration for Children and Families, U.S. Department of Health and Human Services.

Peisner-Feinberg, E. S., Burchinal, M. R., Clifford, R. M., Culkin, M. L., Howes, C., Kagan, S. L., & Yazejian, N. (2001). The relation of preschool child-care quality to children's cognitive and social developmental trajectories through second grade. *Child Development, 72*(5), 1534–1553.

Pianta, R., Howes, C., Burchinal, M., Bryant, D., Clifford, R., Early, D., & Barbarin, O. (2005). Features of pre-kindergarten programs, classrooms, and teachers: Do they predict observed classroom quality and child-teacher interactions? *Applied Developmental Science, 9*(3), 144–159.

Reynolds, A. J., Ou, S., & Temple, J. A. (2018). A multicomponent, preschool to third grade preventive intervention and educational attainment at 35 years of age. *JAMA Pediatrics, 172*(3), 247–256.

Sleeter, C. E. (Ed.). 2007. *Facing accountability in education: Democracy and equity at risk.* New York, NY: Teachers College Press.

U.S. Census Bureau. (2012). *Most children younger than age 1 are minorities.* Retrieved from https://www.census.gov/newsroom/releases/archives/population/cb12-90.html

U.S. Department of Health and Human Services. (n.d.). *Policy statement on early childhood career pathways.* Retrieved from https://www.acf.hhs.gov/ecd/early-childhood-career-pathways

U.S. Department of Health and Human Services and U.S. Department of Education. (2016). *High-quality early learning settings depend on a high-quality workforce: Low compensation undermines quality.* Retrieved from https://www.acf.hhs.gov/ecd/high-quality-early-learning-settings-depend-on-a-high-quality-workforce

Villegas, A. M., & Lucas, T. (2002). *Educating culturally responsive teachers: A coherent approach.* Albany: State University of New York Press.

Vu, J. A., Jeon, H. J., & Howes, C. (2008). Formal education, credential, or both: Early childhood program classroom practices. *Early Education and Development, 19*(3), 479–504.

Washington, V. (2008). *Role, relevance, reinvention: Higher education in the field of early care and education.* Boston, MA: Wheelock College.

Whitebook, M., Bellm, D., Lee, Y., & Sakai, L. (2005). *Time to revamp and expand: Early childhood teacher preparation programs in California's institutions of higher education.* Berkeley, CA: Center for the Study of Child Care Employment, Institute for Research on Labor and Employment, University of California at Berkeley.

Whitebook, M., Gomby, D., Bellm, D., Sakai, L., & Kipnis, F. (2009). *Preparing teachers of young children: The current state of knowledge, and a blueprint for the future. Executive Summary.* Berkeley, CA: Center for the Study of Child Care Employment, Institute for Research on Labor and Employment, University of California at Berkeley.

CHAPTER 11

EDUCATING YOUNG LEARNERS

Future Perspectives

**Sunday O. Obi, Festus E. Obiakor,
Jessica Graves, and Bob Algozzine**

It has become increasingly apparent that one's perception of issues depends largely on his/her personal history. As human beings, professionals and other stakeholders vary in their perspectives, so do they vary on strategies and solutions. Rather than arbitrarily select issues or seek consensus among interdisciplinary but disparate groups, we elected in this chapter to examine the broader array of issues that impact the future educators of young learners, with the aim of conceptualizing effective techniques to reverse problems or difficulties. For instance, many educators have referred to the "cycles" of change in education. These cycles are based on the view that educational perspectives have their time. When they are innovative, they become the status quo, and become finally obsolete as the next group of methods, beliefs, and educational initiatives takes hold.

Special education has been compared to a pendulum (Hewett & Forness, 1977), where beliefs and perspectives swing from the right to the left

Educating Young Children With and Without Exceptionalities, pages 153–163
Copyright © 2019 by Information Age Publishing

and back again. There is evidence that these historical models may have value and help educators to make future predictions based upon the trends of the past. These models demonstrate that change is rarely linear and that modifications and adaptations do not necessarily go in the same direction as the immediate past. The special education pendulum is a reminder that the tide will flow in the opposite direction after it has taken a complete swing. The difficulty of future prediction is not predicting whether things will change (they will), but rather when these changes may occur, and what will result from these changes (Siegel, 1993). Schools are faced with per-petual issues, including who should be served and how and where they should be served. Many, or most, of the issues of today have been issues for well over half a century. One thing is clear, our approaches to these issues may be somewhat more sophisticated today, but we clearly do not yet have the wisdom or the technical knowledge to put these problems behind us.

There are as many issues and trends in special education as there are in regular education. In fact, there is a growing belief that special education is becoming less and less a separate field of interest. Special education has always been concerned with students' individual needs. This philosophy is slowly becoming similar to the goals of general educators. With the prac-tices of integration and inclusion, the line between special education and regular education is becoming increasingly blurry (Siegel, 1993). In this conclusive chapter, we examine historical trends, current issues, and con-sider directions for the future in the education of young learners with and without exceptionalities.

CONCEPTUALIZING INCLUSIVE EDUCATION OF YOUNG LEARNERS

Understanding history is important in every field and endeavor. Santayana's adage that "those who cannot remember the past are condemned to repeat it" is invoked often because it contains more than a grain of truth. In oth-er words, the past shapes the present and future in all aspects of our lives, including special education. Special education has gone through several changes despite being a relatively new field of study. It first received federal regulation and assistance with the passing of the Education for All Handi-capped Children Act of 1975 (aka PL. 94-142). This law required free appro-priate education for all handicapped students and called for the placement of students in the "least restrictive environment." These provisions were the result of growing awareness and advocacy of civil rights and the philosophy of "normalization." Civil rights advocates convinced legislators that children with disabilities should be provided the same educational opportunities as their "able" peers. The normalization philosophy assumes that persons with disabilities want to live as "normally" as possible and schools should assist in this endeavor by integrating students with disabilities with their peers without disabilities. It was believed integration would alleviate prejudice, discrimination, and assist the socialization skills of all involved.

The call for a change came in earnest with inclusive education advocates such as Will (1986) urging general educators to become more responsible for the education of students who have special needs in school, including those who are economically disadvantaged and culturally bilingual. She was supported by many scholars and educators. Constructs and terms like mainstreaming, integration, and the Regular Education Initiative (REI) became very popular. Questions raised by REI advocates soon led to calls for full inclusion. Even though full inclusion has been endorsed by parents and professionals, it has stimulated further debates. Should schools not be about enhancing the quality of life of people and about creating better communities? Should general and special education educators not deal with change while trying to maintain their traditional obligations? Several years ago, the nation's governors, led by then President Bush, agreed on six national educational goals (U.S. Department of Education, 1990). Modified slightly, these goals became the framework for President Clinton's Goals 2000: Educate America Act of 1994 (U.S. Department of Education, 1994). Goals 2000 calls for the education of "all students" including those who are academically talented and those who are culturally and linguistically diverse (CLD) learners with exceptionalities. While progress was being made toward achieving some goals, it was unlikely that the needs of all "normal" and exceptional learners would be met by the turn of the century. The critical question continues to be, "What does the future hold for young children with and without exceptionalities?"

The passage of Public Law (PL) 94-142 improved the educational attention given to persons with disabilities. This law has received several important modifications and revisions over the years of its existence. One key change was the Individuals With Disabilities Education Act or IDEA, the reauthorization that improved the full participation for eligible children with disabilities birth through 21 by providing funds to states to assist them in developing and implementing systems of early intervention and special education and related services for all eligible infants and toddlers and children and youth with disabilities. The IDEA Part C program requires that eligible infants and toddlers with disabilities receive services in natural environments to the maximum extent appropriate and the IDEA Part B program requires that eligible children with disabilities age three through 21 receiving services in the least restrictive environment (LRE) to the maximum extent appropriate. Eligible children with disabilities under Part B of the IDEA are to receive the full range of supplementary aids and services to enable them to be educated with children who do not have disabilities, participate in the general educational or developmental curriculum, and participate in typical nonacademic activities with peers without disabilities, to the maximum extent appropriate.

SUCCESSES AND CHALLENGES IN SPECIAL EDUCATION

In conjunction with the No Child Left Behind Act (NCLB) of 2002, the IDEA stipulated that educators in public schools must use a variety of accommodations and modifications to remove learning barriers for children with disabilities. As indicated, the IDEA covers a wide variety of disabilities. The classification of a student's special needs, as well as the stipulations in his or her IEP, dictates the best way to help that child overcome barriers to learning and have a greater chance for a successful learning experience. To be successful in implementing full inclusion for every young child, the family and the child with special needs will need additional support personnel when in a regular education or recreational program. Staffing, class size, number of children with disabilities, and the nature and quality of a child's disability are important factors. Ideally, the number of children with special needs in a classroom should approach the distribution in society, where approximately 1 out of 15 American children has a disability. This increases the opportunity for children to get to know and appreciate one another without overwhelming the capacity of teachers and students (Astor, 2017). Inclusion is a value, much like the commitment to racial or gender equality. It may not always be easy. It may require change and accommodation, but the process of inclusion and the encouragement of each individual child allows each person to develop his or her talents and strengths. It also provides opportunities for all professionals and stakeholders to develop the much-desired qualities of compassion, empathy, and helpfulness. In the end, it can teach every child that the greater the diversity, the richer our capacity to create a more humane and respectful society.

Presently, contemporary special education is approaching some particularly critical crossroads, with significant changes in policy and practice being considered. For example, response to intervention (RTI) and multitiered systems of support (MTSS) reforms represent fundamentally new approaches for identifying and educating young learners with and at risk for disabilities. Additionally, students with individualized education plans (IEPs) are being included in standard-based reforms (e.g., state proficiency tests and Common Core State Standards) and are expected to participate in the general education curriculum. And, special educators are increasingly asked to support the inclusion of students with disabilities through co-teaching, which represents new roles and responsibilities for special and general educators.

Despite all advances and successes in special education and the young learners who have derived benefits from it, special education budgets face constant scrutiny from government leaders. One budget cut proposed in 2012 could have adversely affected more than 6 million students with special needs and resulted in layoffs of more than 10,000 special education teachers and other support staff. However, in September 2015, U.S. Department of Education and Health and Human Services issued a policy statement on promoting inclusion in early childhood programs and provide recommendations to states, local educational agencies (LEAs), schools, and public and private early childhood programs (U.S. Department of Education, 2015). On January 9, 2017, the U.S. Department of Education, Office of Special Education and Rehabilitative Services wrote a "Dear Colleague Letter" (DCL) to reaffirm the position of the U.S. Department of Education that all young children with disabilities should have access to inclusive high-quality early childhood programs where they are provided with individualized and appropriate supports to enable them to meet high expectations. In fact, despite waning resources, outdated assessment and needed funding, special education thrives and continues to evolve along with technology.

It is apparent that the aforementioned provisions will advance the well-being of exceptional children. As indicated earlier, special education is governed by state statutes as well as the federal laws to provide opportunities to millions of individuals with disabilities. To continue the progress in the field of special education, the Every Student Succeeds Act (ESSA) was signed by President Obama on December 10, 2015 and represented good news for our nation's schools. This bipartisan measure reauthorized the 50-year-old Elementary and Secondary Education Act (ESEA), the nation's national education law and longstanding commitment to equal opportunity for all students. The new law built on key areas of progress in recent years, made possible by the efforts of educators, communities, parents, and students across the country. For example, recent high school graduation rates are at all-time highs. Dropout rates are at historic lows. And, more students are going to college than ever before. These achievements provide a firm foundation for further work to expand educational opportunities and improve student outcomes under ESSA.

The earlier version of ESSA, the No Child Left Behind (NCLB) Act, was enacted in 2002. NCLB represented a significant step forward for our nation's children in many respects, particularly as it shined a light on where students were making progress and where they needed additional support, regardless of race, income, zip code, disability, home language, or background. The law was scheduled for revision and, over time, NCLB's prescriptive requirements became increasingly unworkable for schools and educators. Recognizing this fact, in 2010, the Obama administration joined a call from educators and families to create a better law that focused on the clear goal of fully preparing all students for success in college and careers. Congress responded to that call by passing the ESSA in 2015 to ensure success for students and schools. Some provisions of this law are:

- Advance equity by upholding critical protections for America's disadvantaged and high-need students.
- Require for the first time that all students in America be taught with high academic standards that will prepare them to succeed in college and careers.
- Ensure that vital information is provided to educators, families, students, and communities through annual statewide assessments that measure students' progress toward those high standards.
- Help to support and grow local innovations, including evidence-based and place-based interventions developed by local leaders and educators consistent with the "Investing in Innovation" (http://www2.ed.gov/programs/innovation/index.html) and "Promise Neighborhoods" programs (http://www2.ed.gov/programs/promiseneighborhoods/index.html).
- Sustain and expand this administration's historic investments in increasing access to high-quality preschool (http://www.ed.gov/early-learning).
- Maintain an expectation that there will be accountability and action to effect positive change in our lowest-performing schools, where groups of students are not making progress, and where graduation rates are low over extended periods of time.

Furthermore, the ESSA was launched with the publication of a policy statement by the U.S. Department of Health and Human Services and the U.S. Department of Education (2015)—"The Policy Statement on the Inclusion of Children With Disabilities in Early Childhood Programs." The purpose was to set a vision and provide recommendations to states, local educational agencies (LEAs), schools, and public and private early childhood programs. In addition, the intention was to increase the inclusion of infants, toddlers, and preschool children with disabilities in high-quality early childhood programs. More specifically, the policy statement continues to acknowledge that all young children with disabilities should have access to high-quality inclusive settings and maintain high expectations. The policy statement specifically called for the use of embedded instruction, scaffolding, and tiered models of instruction.

Great interest in how to deliver effective instruction to all children (including those with disabilities) has grown because many of the quality initiatives focus on providing services in inclusive settings and improving social and pre-academic outcomes. The placement of children with disabilities in these programs does not ensure that they will reach high standards. The Council for Exceptional Children's Division for Early Childhood (DEC) and the National Association for the Education of Young Children (NAEYC) published a joint position statement in 2009 (DEC/NAEYC, 2009) in which they identified three defining features of inclusion—*access, participation, and supports.* Children with disabilities must be included in preschool programs and given effective instruction so they can reach high standards (Barton & Smith, 2015; DEC, 2014; Odom, Buysse, & Soukakou, 2011; Schwartz et al., 2002; Strain & Bovey, 2011).

For these children to receive individualized supports they need to thrive, these require a community-wide partnership that brings families, advocates and self-advocates, developmental specialists, early childhood programs, schools, LEAs, and community and state leaders together to build a culture of inclusion, supported by empirical and legal foundations of inclusion. Though these efforts have been underway in communities for many years, they need to be expanded and more widely adopted across the country. These efforts will require partners to come together to:

- Celebrate diversity of all forms and in all facets of society.
- Talk to neighbors, community members, and state and local leaders about the importance of inclusion; highlight the universal benefits of inclusion for children with and without disabilities; and counter myths, misconceptions, and about children with disabilities.
- Co-create inclusion strategic plans at state, LEA, and school levels.
- Strongly communicate inclusion as a shared responsibility and a top priority and demonstrate a commitment to inclusion through policy changes and appropriate resource allocation at all levels.

A central component of establishing a culture of inclusion within the school system is ensuring that individualized needs, supports, expectations, and goals of children with disabilities are always considered with those of other children. It is critical for all programs to consider the principles of *access, participation,* and *support.* As defined in the DEC/NAEYC (2009) inclusion position statement, *access* refers to removing structural, physical, or communicative-related barriers to full participation; *participation* refers to strategies used to promote children's learning, development, and sense of belonging; and *support* refers to the broader system that enables these efforts, including program/school-family partnerships and professional development. Systems should be designed in ways that are beneficial to all children in their communities.

FUTURE PERSPECTIVES

Much has been accomplished in terms of making special education available to children with disabilities. Educators and school leaders have learned much about how to effectively teach children who are at risk for misidentification, misassessment, misintegration/mislabeling, misplacement, and mis-instruction (Obiakor, 1999, 2001, 2007, 2018; Obiakor, Banks, Rotatori, & Utley, 2017) Special educators and families are learning to work as partners on behalf of exceptional children. Technological advances have helped many students overcome challenges (e.g., students with physical impairments and communication disabilities). Of the many challenges the special education field faces, none is more critical than getting effective teaching practices effectively implemented. More specifically, special education must reduce the gap between what scientific research tells us about effective teaching practice and what children with exceptionalities experience in the classroom. General and special educators must understand how to provide an education that gives equal opportunity to students regardless of gender, socioeconomic status, ethnic group, disability, or other cultural identity. In doing so, the underrepresentation or overrepresentation of some ethnic minorities in certain special education categories will be eliminated. It is said that some students with disabilities still experience discrimination or receive a less than adequate education because of their race, ethnicity, social class, or other differences from the majority (Heward, 1996; Obiakor, 1999, 2001, 2007, 2018; Obiakor et al., 2017).

Working toward an ideal society demands a multicultural perspective, understanding and accepting one another's cultures, and seeing diversity as strength rather than a fatal flaw. Diversity should not be a reason for disability. Moreover, educators who do not have the knowledge of what to do are already having severe problems in general and special education programs. As it appears, there is a great lack of qualified teachers, and often, principals are forced to employ teachers who are not trained educators. Teacher education should better prepare students in order to meet the needs of the variation of all children. Changes such as an increase in diverse family and living situations, nontraditional employment and the resulting need for extended hours of special care, and increasing economic inequality among families require innovative solutions and innovative preparation. Many special education teachers in the field are inadequately prepared and receive minimal support (Kauffman, 1999, 2000; Blanton, Pugach, & Boveda, 2014). According to Kauffman (2000), what has happened in the preparation of teachers and leadership personnel should shock us into unhappiness. Frantic steps must be taken to address inadequate teacher preparation, perpetual teacher shortage, and widespread teacher attrition. Reducing the demand for special education teachers by including more students in general education settings is not a good strategy for addressing the special education shortage. Few would argue against full inclusion if the educational needs of all students with disabilities could be met appropriately in general education settings (Hallahan & Kauffman, 2000). Unfortunately, for students with disabilities, opportunities for academic and social success do not exist in general education settings.

CONCLUSION

For a brighter future, special education must continue to provide an education that gives equal opportunities to young students regardless of gender, socioeconomic status, ethnic group, disability, or other cultural identity. While special education's identity has weakened in some places, special education has continued to create opportunities for those with special needs. The good news is that in the past decade, and especially in the years since the introduction of IDEA 2004 and ESSA 2015, major shifts have been and are taking place in the United States for students with disabilities. We believe special education will continue to apply more powerful versions of assessment and instruction for young learners. As a result, change appears inevitable if the quality of education for students with special needs is to be improved. More specifically, our future could be made brighter by focusing on instruction, demanding and following scientific evidence, preparing manuals and checklists for teachers based on scientific evidence, making students' sustained success our primary objective, and thinking and talking more carefully about what special education is and does. We acknowledge that threats external to special education certainly exist, but internal threats are most likely to injure or kill the field. Special education has needlessly, sometimes unwittingly, gouged itself and now seems to threaten its own life (Kauffman, 2014). We need general and special education that do not discriminate, misidentify, misassess, mislabel/miscategorize, misplace, and misinstruct (Obiakor, 1999, 2001, 2007, 2018; Obiakor et al., 2017). Simply put, we need general and special education that work. In the end, we must be forward-looking and optimistic—The fields of general and special education have much to offer all learners, especially our young children.

REFERENCES

Astor, S. (2017). *Inclusion: Doing our best for all children*. Des Moines, IA: Meredith Corporation.

Barton, E. E., & Smith, B. J. (2015). *The pre-school inclusion toolbox*. Baltimore, MD: Paul H. Brookes.

Blanton, L. P., Pugach, M. C., & Boveda, M. (2014). *Teacher education reform initiatives and special education: Convergence, divergence, and missed opportunities* (Document No. LS-3). Retrieved from University of Florida, Collaboration for Effective Educator, Development, Accountability, and Reform Center website: http://ceedar.education.ufl.edu/wp-content/uploads/2014/09/LS-3_FINAL_09-20-14.pdf

DEC/NAEYC. (2009). *Early childhood inclusion: A joint position statement of the Division for Early Childhood (DEC) and the National Association for the Education of Young Children (NAEYC).* Chapel Hill: The University of North Carolina, FPG Child Development Institute.

Division for Early Childhood. (2014). *DEC recommended practices in early intervention/ early childhood special education 2014.* Retrieved from http://www.dec-sped.org/recommendedpractices

Hallahan, D. P., & Kauffman, J. M. (2000). *Exceptional learners: Introduction to special education* (8th ed.). Boston, MA: Allyn & Bacon.

Heward, W. L. (1996). *Exceptional children: An introduction to special education* (5th ed.). Englewood Cliffs, NJ: Merrill/Prentice Hall.

Hewett, F., & Forness, S. (1977). *Education of exceptional learners.* Boston, MA: Allyn & Bacon.

Kauffman, J. M. (1999). Commentary: Today's special education and its messages for tomorrow. *The Journal of Special Education, 32*(4), 244–254.

Kauffman, J. M. (2000). The special education story: Obituary, accident report, conversion experience, reincarnation, or none of the above. *Exceptionality, 8*(1), 61–71.

Kauffman, J. M. (2014). Past, present, and future in EBD and special education. In B. G. Cook, M. Tankersley, & T. J. Landrum (Eds.), *Advances in learning and behavioral disabilities, 27-Special Education, past, present, and future: Perspectives from the field* (pp. 63–87). Bingley, England: Emerald.

Obiakor, F. E. (1999). Teacher expectations of minority exceptional learners: Impact on "accuracy" of self-concepts. *Exceptional Children, 66*(1), 39–53.

Obiakor, F. E. (2001). *It even happens in "good" schools: Responding to cultural diversity in today's classrooms.* Thousand Oaks, CA: Corwin Press.

Obiakor, F. E. (2007). Multicultural special education: Effective intervention for today's schools. *Intervention in School and Clinic, 42*(3), 148–155.

Obiakor, F. E. (2018). *Powerful multifunctional essays for innovational educators and leaders: Optimizing "hearty" conversations.* Charlotte, NC: Information Age.

Obiakor, F. E., Banks, T., Rotatori, A. F., & Utley, C. (2017). *Leadership matters in the education of students with special needs in the 21st century.* Charlotte, NC: Information Age.

Odom, S. L., Buysse, V., & Soukakou, E. (2011). Inclusion for young children with disabilities: A quarter century of research perspectives. *Journal of Early Intervention, 33*(4), 344–356.

Schwartz, I., Sandall, S., Odom, S., Horn, E., & Beckman, P. (2002). I know it when I see it: In search of a common definition of inclusion. In S. L. Odom (Ed.), *Widening the circle: Including children with disabilities in preschool programs* (pp. 10–24). New York, NY: Teachers College Press.

Siegel, J. (1993). *Special education issues, trends and future predictions.* Portales, New Mexico: ERIC Document Reproduction Service. (EC302415)

Strain, P. S., & Bovey, E. H. (2011). Randomized, controlled trial of the LEAP model of early intervention for young children with autism spectrum disorders. *Topics in Early Childhood Special Education, 31*(3), 133–154.

U.S. Department of Education. (1990). *National goals for education.* Washington, DC: U.S. Government Printing Office.

U.S. Department of Education. (1994). *Sixteenth annual report to congress on the implementation of the Individuals With Disabilities Education Act.* Washington, DC: U.S. Government Printing Office.

U.S. Department of Health and Human Services and U. S. Department of Education. (2015). *Policy statement on inclusion of children with disabilities in early childhood programs.* Retrieved from https://ed.gov/policy/speced/guid/early learning/joint-statement-full-text.pdf

Will, M. C. (1986). Educating children with learning problems: A shared responsibility. *Exceptional Children, 52*(5), 411–415.

Made in the USA
Monee, IL
03 February 2020